OPPOSING
VIEWPOINTS®
SERIES

Global Resources

Other Books of Related Interest:

Opposing Viewpoints Series

Energy Alternatives

Food

Oil

Current Controversies Series

Alternative Energy Sources

Food

Globalization

At Issue Series

Is the World Heading Toward an Energy Crisis?

Managing America's Forests

Rain Forests

Will the World Run Out of Fresh Water?

World Hunger

"Congress shall make
no law . . . abridging
the freedom of speech,
or of the press."

First Amendment to the U.S. Constitution

The basic foundation of our democracy is the First Amendment guarantee of freedom of expression. The Opposing Viewpoints Series is dedicated to the concept of this basic freedom and the idea that it is more important to practice it than to enshrine it.

OPPOSING VIEWPOINTS® SERIES

Global Resources

Clare Hanrahan, Book Editor

GREENHAVEN PRESS

An imprint of Thomson Gale, a part of The Thomson Corporation

THOMSON

™

GALE

Detroit • New York • San Francisco • New Haven, Conn. • Waterville, Maine • London

Christine Nasso, *Publisher*
Elizabeth Des Chenes, *Managing Editor*

© 2008 The Gale Group.

Star logo is a trademark and Gale and Greenhaven Press are registered trademarks used herein under license.

For more information, contact:
Greenhaven Press
27500 Drake Rd.
Farmington Hills, MI 48331-3535
Or you can visit our Internet site at http://www.gale.com

LIBRARY OF CONGRESS CATALOGING-IN-PUBLICATION DATA

Global resources / David M. Haugen, book editor.
    p. cm. -- (Opposing viewpoints)
    Includes bibliographical references and index.
ISBN 978-0-7377-3743-1 (hardcover)
    ISBN 978-0-7377-3744-8 (pbk.)
    1. Natural resources. I. Haugen, David M., 1969-.
    HC85.G58 2008
    333.7--dc22

                                                    2007038577

Printed in the United States of America
10 9 8 7 6 5 4 3 2 1

Contents

Chapter 3: What Alternative Energy Sources Are Worth Pursuing?

Chapter 4: How Can the World's Resources Be Preserved?

Why Consider Opposing Viewpoints?

> *"The only way in which a human being can make some approach to knowing the whole of a subject is by hearing what can be said about it by persons of every variety of opinion and studying all modes in which it can be looked at by every character of mind. No wise man ever acquired his wisdom in any mode but this."*
>
> *John Stuart Mill*

In our media-intensive culture it is not difficult to find differing opinions. Thousands of newspapers and magazines and dozens of radio and television talk shows resound with differing points of view. The difficulty lies in deciding which opinion to agree with and which "experts" seem the most credible. The more inundated we become with differing opinions and claims, the more essential it is to hone critical reading and thinking skills to evaluate these ideas. Opposing Viewpoints books address this problem directly by presenting stimulating debates that can be used to enhance and teach these skills. The varied opinions contained in each book examine many different aspects of a single issue. While examining these conveniently edited opposing views, readers can develop critical thinking skills such as the ability to compare and contrast authors' credibility, facts, argumentation styles, use of persuasive techniques, and other stylistic tools. In short, the Opposing Viewpoints series is an ideal way to attain the higher-level thinking and reading skills so essential in a culture of diverse and contradictory opinions.

In addition to providing a tool for critical thinking, Opposing Viewpoints books challenge readers to question their own strongly held opinions and assumptions. Most people form their opinions on the basis of upbringing, peer pressure, and personal, cultural, or professional bias. By reading carefully balanced opposing views, readers must directly confront new ideas as well as the opinions of those with whom they disagree. This is not to simplistically argue that everyone who reads opposing views will—or should—change his or her opinion. Instead, the series enhances readers' understanding of their own views by encouraging confrontation with opposing ideas. Careful examination of others' views can lead to the readers' understanding of the logical inconsistencies in their own opinions, perspective on why they hold an opinion, and the consideration of the possibility that their opinion requires further evaluation.

Evaluating Other Opinions

To ensure that this type of examination occurs, Opposing Viewpoints books present all types of opinions. Prominent spokespeople on different sides of each issue as well as well-known professionals from many disciplines challenge the reader. An additional goal of the series is to provide a forum for other, less known, or even unpopular viewpoints. The opinion of an ordinary person who has had to make the decision to cut off life support from a terminally ill relative, for example, may be just as valuable and provide just as much insight as a medical ethicist's professional opinion. The editors have two additional purposes in including these less known views. One, the editors encourage readers to respect others' opinions—even when not enhanced by professional credibility. It is only by reading or listening to and objectively evaluating others' ideas that one can determine whether they are worthy of consideration. Two, the inclusion of such viewpoints encourages the important critical thinking skill of objectively evaluating an author's credentials and bias. This evaluation will illuminate an author's reasons for taking a particular stance on an issue and will aid in readers' evaluation of the author's ideas.

It is our hope that these books will give readers a deeper understanding of the issues debated and an appreciation of the complexity of even seemingly simple issues when good and honest people disagree. This awareness is particularly important in a democratic society such as ours in which people enter into public debate to determine the common good. Those with whom one disagrees should not be regarded as enemies but rather as people whose views deserve careful examination and may shed light on one's own.

Thomas Jefferson once said that "difference of opinion leads to inquiry, and inquiry to truth." Jefferson, a broadly educated man, argued that "if a nation expects to be ignorant and free . . . it expects what never was and never will be." As individuals and as a nation, it is imperative that we consider the opinions of others and examine them with skill and discernment. The Opposing Viewpoints series is intended to help readers achieve this goal.

David L. Bender and Bruno Leone,
Founders

Introduction

"Overconsumption by the wealthiest fifth of humanity is an environmental problem unmatched in severity by anything but perhaps population growth. The surging exploitation of resources threatens to exhaust or unalterably disfigure forests, soils, water, air, and climate."

"Of course, underconsumption—poverty—is no solution. Poverty is infinitely worse for people and bad for the natural world, too. Dispossessed peasants slash-and-burn their way into the rain forests of Latin America, and hungry nomads turn their herds out onto fragile African rangeland, reducing it to desert."

"If environmental decline results when people have either too little or too much, we must ask ourselves: How much is enough? What level of consumption can the earth support? When does consumption cease to add appreciably to human satisfaction?"

> Alan Durning,
> The Futurist

Since 1993, ecologists and demographers have utilized a simple mathematical formula to determine how many hectares (1 hectare=2.47 acres) of land and water are needed to create and regenerate the resources consumed by a given population. The resulting measurement is called an ecological footprint, and it can be used to determine consumption on a personal, local, national, or global scale.

According to the Global Footprint Network, an ecological organization that promotes the wise use of the planet's resources, the countries of the world currently cast a footprint that is 23 percent larger than its biocapacity (i.e., what the earth can sustain). However, not all nations are equally to blame for demanding more from the earth than it can securely supply. Most countries are running an "ecological deficit" (meaning they consume more than they can supply), but only a few are egregious overconsumers. The United States, Japan, India, China, and many European nations claim three-quarters of the world's resources, leaving the rest of the world—largely composed of developing countries—to subsist on the remaining quarter. In the United States alone, the per capita use of resources is more than five times the sustainable global level of 1.8 hectares per person.

The overconsumption of resources is worrisome for those who believe that the sustainable management of the planet's biocapacity is the only way to avert disasters such as famine, the collapse of fisheries, and the depletion of fossil fuels. Some analysts, however, predict that unsustainable practices will have more than just environmental consequences. In 2006, British Defense Secretary John Reid warned that the hoarding of resources would lead to violent conflict on an international—and perhaps worldwide—scale. He argued that global warming—itself a product of rapid resource consumption—was already desiccating arable land and contributing to water crises and would "make the emergence of violent conflict more rather than less likely."

Reid's supposition has some historical support. In October 2001, Paul Collier and Anke Hoeffler, two members of the Centre for the Study of African Economies (CSAE), reviewed fifty-four civil wars that occurred between 1965 and 1999.

They concluded that the more a country depends on exporting primary resources for its gross national product, the higher the risk of conflict. Especially vulnerable were oil-rich nations in Africa, such as Nigeria, Sudan, and the Congo. The Congo is an exceptional case because it has also suffered civil conflict over deposits of cobalt, copper, diamonds, gold, and timber. Michael Renner, a senior researcher with Worldwatch Institute in Washington, estimates that more than 5 million people lost their lives in various "resource wars" in the 1990s alone. Renner, in fact, believes that it is the abundance of natural resources, not their dearth, that is fueling most resource conflicts in the current century.

Although some of the civil wars in the last half-century have been waged by various interest groups protecting local resource supplies (such as fresh water), many have been instigated in order to seize scarce resources that have value in global markets. Some critics, such as John Gray of the London School of Economics, maintain that free market trade has been a primary contributor to resource exploitation. In his 2003 book, *Al Qaeda and What It Means to Be Modern*, Gray argues that free trade is predicated on a positivist philosophy, namely that "if demand exceeds supply, resources will become expensive. As a result, new supplies will be found—or technological alternatives developed." This belief, Gray states, has never fit well with the reality of scarcity. Industrial states failed to provide alternatives to oil and other resources and instead turned to hoarding. Gray insists that the globalization policies of industrialized nations and international corporations are designed to provide these entities with access to scarce resources within the borders of less developed countries.

There are several solutions to the present inequalities in resource distribution. Some observers suggest the equitable sharing of the world's remaining resources, so that each nation is entitled to a fair portion. The international organization Share the World's Resources, for example, asserts that "the essentials for life must be cooperatively owned and managed by the global public, and shared internationally according to need under the guidance of a reformed United Nations. Such resources include energy, food, water, healthcare, education and technology." Other analysts believe the emphasis should not necessarily be on sharing resources but sustaining those regenerative resources that are being overconsumed.

The concept of sustainable development has been touted since the late 1980s and links resource exploitation with other major global problems such as poverty, hunger, disease, and environmental degradation. Remedying overconsumption will require addressing these other problems as a whole, advocates contend. But some strategies can be used directly to reduce the strain on natural resources and reduce the ecological footprints of most nations. These include recycling woods and precious metals, reusing water, and exploring alternative energy sources. By focusing on preserving limited resources in these ways, sustainable development hopes to protract the life of resources and keep them around for future generations.

The United Nations (UN) has already created policies to promote sustainable development, but it has yet to find a means to overcome national sovereignty. For example, in its 1992 Earth Summit in Rio de Janeiro, Brazil, the UN adopted a declaration that stated that nations have a right to develop and to exploit their own resources as long as the exploitation does not do ecological harm to the global environment. Thus, nations are still left in control of their own resources and can drain them if it suits their own interests. While this concession seems to be antithetical to the aims of global sustainable development, it was included to appease the signatory nations that otherwise believed their own property would be taken from them and doled out to the world.

This fear of loss of property rights is one of the reasons that critics oppose sustainable development. The American free-market organization Freedom 21 claims that "for progress to be made in implementing Sustainable Development in the United States, unalienable rights such as the right to property must be eroded, attacked, and struck down altogether." Such groups see planned development as a redistribution of wealth and as a blow to private enterprise. Positivists of a sort, they place their faith in the market, believing that private enterprise will respond accordingly to resource scarcity and the problems of overconsumption when consumers—not governments or partisan collectives—push for change.

The authors of the viewpoints in *Opposing Viewpoints: Global Resources* debate proposed strategies for limiting the ecological footprint of humankind. In a chapter entitled "How Can the World's Resources Be Preserved?" commentators address the contentions between free trade and sustainable development, while in the chapter "Are Global Resources Overstrained?" some critics take issue with the notion that scarcity is even as problematic as commonly believed. In the remaining two chapters, "What Global Agricultural Policies Should Be Pursued?" and "What Alternative Energy Sources Are Worth Pursuing?" analysts debate the alternatives to current practices of providing enough food and energy for a world population that is still expanding and will likely consume even more resources as it grows. All of these chapters and the viewpoints within them dissect the twin concerns of global resources and global consumption in an effort to better understand if the people of the world can balance what they need with what the earth can provide.

CHAPTER 1

Are Global Resources Overstrained?

Chapter Preface

In mid-2007, the global population reached 6.6 billion people—a number more than twice the world's population just 50 years ago. The U.S. Census Bureau expects that by the year 2042, the figure will rise by another 3 billion people, with much of the growth occurring in developing nations where resources to support such growth are scarce. The rate of growth may be slowing, but the overall increase scares many who believe the world cannot support such vast numbers of human beings indefinitely.

In *An Essay on the Principle of Population*, the eighteenth-century English demographer Thomas Malthus warned that the exponential growth of human population would soon outstrip the food resources of the planet, leading to famine and other dire social ills in the nineteenth century. Malthus's logic, however, was constrained by pre-industrial-era thinking, and his predictions did not come to pass as succeeding decades witnessed the invention of fertilizers, better farming equipment, and high-yield crops. Even in modern times, though, other observers have taken up the Malthusian cry and noted that industrial processes have added to other problems such as global warming that could negatively impact food crops and lead to the kinds of food shortages Malthus predicted.

One of the more notable modern books to follow the path of Malthusian thinking is *Limits to Growth*, written by environmentalist Donella Meadows and three colleagues. In this 1972 book, the authors used a computer model to predict the impact of population growth on food as well as other global resources. They concluded that various precious metals would be depleted by 1990 and that oil would exhausted by 1992. Like those of Thomas Malthus, these prophecies did not prove accurate. Yet even if these worldwide depletions have not occurred, observers still warn of other looming catastrophes.

Robert Svadlenka of the global hunger and poverty organization World Hunger Year maintains that water shortages will foment serious global crisis in coming decades. He states that 29 nations currently face water shortages and that half the world's lakes and rivers are imperiled by pollution. Claiming that poor water management (including lack of water recovery, wasteful irrigation, and unchecked degradation of water supplies) is behind the crisis, he asserts, "If the current inefficient and destructive practices of water utilization are allowed to continue in the face of growing population, global water resource limits will be reached in a few decades." Svadlenka also reaches the logical conclusion that a shortage of water will likely increase food scarcity in many parts of the world as irrigation sources either dry up or are so severely degraded as to be useless.

Not every prognosticator fears that population growth will overtax the planet's resources. As some of the commentators in chapter 1 suggest, the proper management and distribution of food and water resources may ensure that the dire events predicted by others do not occur. No one can be sure whether the students of Malthus will have their assumptions disproved by human invention, or whether the incompatibility between a growing world population and limited global resources will lead to an inescapable Malthusian end.

"The last great oil frontiers were found almost four decades ago."

The Depletion of Oil Reserves Is a Global Problem

Matthew Simmons

Matthew Simmons is the chairman of Simmons & Company International, an energy investment banking firm. In the following viewpoint, he argues that a global energy crisis is likely to occur because of the world's dependence on rapidly depleting fossil fuels. He maintains that large oil fields are drying up, and their output has dropped significantly in recent years. Simmons fears that the rising demand for oil and gas will eventually create shortages that could be disastrous for the world's economy and increase tensions in already unstable parts of the globe.

As you read, consider the following questions:

1. According to Simmons, how many giant oil fields are there in the world?

2. As Simmons notes, how many barrels of oil do prediction models estimate will be needed per day to satisfy global demands between 2020 and 2030?

Matthew Simmons, "Shock to the System: The Impending Global Energy Supply Crisis," *Harvard International Review*, vol. 28, no. 3, Fall 2006. Copyright © 2006 *The Harvard International Review*. Reproduced by permission.

3. In what year does the Association for the Study of
Peak Oil predict a peak of sustainable supply?

For decades our conception of a serious global economic threat has been limited to wars or financial disasters. The possibility of energy issues morphing into economic disruptions faded as the world enjoyed decades of low energy prices and ample supplies. Over time, the energy worries that deeply concerned many public policy planners in 1973 and again in 1979 to 1981 became distant memories. The handful of serious energy students who warned of pending problems were usually dismissed by most energy economists and labeled as pessimists, contrarians, or alarmists crying wolf.

Unfortunately, the risk that the world might suddenly face a massive energy crisis never disappeared, even as oil and gas supplies grew from many new sources. Over the last three decades, the risk of a severe energy crisis crept inexorably closer as demand for oil and gas steadily grew while the supply of oil and gas matured. New discoveries of oil and gas over the last four decades were minute in comparison to early ones and were often from poor quality reservoirs. A growing percentage of world oil and gas supplies came from countries prone to political instability.

Since access to supplies of oil and gas underpins almost every aspect of modern society, there is perhaps no greater threat to the global economy than demand surging ahead of supply and triggering physical shortages. Only a massive war, pandemic, or global water shortage would inflict as severe a jolt to the world.

The Myth of Abundant Oil

For the past 50 years, the world has blissfully assumed that oil and gas supplies were abundant and inexpensive to produce. Anchoring this cheap energy thesis were the belief that known Middle East oil reserves would last for 50 to 90 years and the

comforting thought that most of the Middle East had barely
been explored. Moreover, conventional wisdom assumed that
producing Middle East oil was virtually costless. Thus, the
only two major "risks" that worried energy observers were
that a glut of cheap Middle East oil would wipe out supplies
from safer regions or that geopolitical unrest would keep
some supply from the market.

For some inexplicable reason, virtually no energy planner
ever questioned this "Middle East Energy Abundance Theory,"
though little hard data, audited by third-party experts, ever
existed to confirm it. For the past 50 years, the theory that
Middle East oil was virtually inexhaustible was discussed so
often in energy circles that it became codified into an "Energy
Fact" needing no further proof.

What most energy observers missed was some basic information about the fragility of both Middle East oil and Middle
East natural gas, documented in hundreds of technical papers.
These were not necessarily easily to read and grasp quickly,
but none were locked up in a secret vault.

Fewer than 40 giant and super giant oil fields have ever
been discovered in almost 100 years of intense Middle East
exploration for oil and gas. These comprise a significant portion of the world's roughly 120 giant oil fields. Of these, the
14 largest account for roughly 20 percent of all oil production.

These giant Middle East oil and gas fields were lined up
like a convoy of tankers along both sides of the Persian Gulf.
From the furthest northern field, Kirkuk, at the top of Iraq,
there is a "golden energy triangle" extending about 1,100 miles
to the eastern side of the Persian Gulf. The triangle's bottom
leg extends 450 miles across the United Arab Emirates and the
top of Oman. Its final leg goes back up to the triangle's top,
just west of the Saudi Arabian side of the Gulf. Within this

triangle reside virtually all the Middle East's giant oil and gas fields that have been supplying the world with inexpensive oil for 35 to 80 years.

The End of "Easy" Oil Supplies

The high-quality light oil coming from some of the most productive reservoir rocks ever discovered is now rapidly being depleted. A high percentage of what were once key Middle East crude grades now come from shrunken sources. Current production targets in countries like Saudi Arabia and Kuwait are tapping pockets of oil left behind from the massive water injection program designed to sweep out all the "easy" oil these great fields could produce. Other new sources of oil supply are from thin oil "streaks" or oil being produced from very tight rocks or a combination of both.

The Golden Age of abundant and cheap Middle East oil is long gone. Middle East oil is now facing its Twilight Era. Saudi Arabia's great oil reserves are increasingly scarce: seven key fields produce 90 percent of Saudi oil, but the "sweet spots" of each of these fields are almost depleted. Abqaiq, the third-largest Saudi field, is now relying for its key extraction on previously bypassed "pockets" of oil. Current rates of decline approximate 8 percent each year, and spare production capacity has dropped from more than 5 million barrels per day in 2002 to less than 1 million [in 2006].

Middle East gas, also thought to be in vast supply, has barely been drilled, but the results to date indicate gas that is often sour and from very tight or ultra tight rocks. The sustainability and growth of Middle East natural gas is shrouded in secrecy, but the limited information in the public domain on key gas fields does not bode well.

A large percentage of the world's oil and gas supplies outside the Middle East also come from large fields now too old and new fields that are too small. The technology developed to find and extract oil merely allowed small fields to be exploited and oil and gas to be extracted at far faster rates. Technology did to a small extent enable the recovery of more oil and gas, but it did so mainly by "managing the tail end of a field's production"—allowing an almost depleted old oil field to continue to produce small volumes for an extended period. Clearly, this method has no long-term prospects.

Rising Demand for Oil

Nonetheless, the world's energy consumers have blithely assumed their energy use could grow exponentially. No one warned them to curb their energy appetite. Forty years ago, when the world used only half the oil it uses now, global oil use was primarily confined to the USSR, Western Europe, the United States, and Japan. By 2006 every country embraces vehicles and lifestyles once only enjoyed in the world's wealthy countries. This change created an inexhaustible growth in oil demand. The various models forecasting oil demand by 2020 to 2030 all end up showing a world needing between 115 and 130 million barrels a day of oil use and demand for natural gas, 50 percent higher than today.

As astonishing as these demand forecasts sound, the estimates are based on relatively conservative assumptions: population growth will slow down, the global economy will become increasingly energy efficient, and developing countries like China and India will use far less oil and gas per capita by 2030 than a poor country like Mexico uses now.

Regardless of how conservative these forecasts for oil and gas demand might be, there is little chance that growth of any magnitude can occur. There is one energy rule that will never change: energy use cannot exceed available supply.

Given the rapid growth in demand for gas and oil, and the way many developing countries are rapidly mimicking South Korea or Singapore's economic growth over the past 20 years, the risk is high that energy demand for oil and gas will soon surge ahead of available supply. This will lead to energy shortages. Shortages encourage energy consumers to hoard, which in turn sends demand surging even higher.

Those who argue that this scenario is far too pessimistic depend upon a general hunch that new technology and high energy prices will soon yield vast new energy supplies. But this has been debated for almost a decade and so far, no groundbreaking technology has been developed to improve extraction and expand reserves. The last great oil frontiers were found almost four decades ago.

The Peak of Oil Supplies Is Imminent

Energy planners now need to grasp the high risk that the world's supply of both oil and gas is fast approaching its highest sustained peak supply. If this is true, stretching supply further now will naturally cause it to fall more drastically once the peak is reached. Unfortunately, rosy projections, like those of the U.S. Energy Information Administration, suggest that oil production is unlikely to peak for several decades. Such optimistic forecasts often reflect the assumption that technological improvements will continuously enlarge reserves and allow more oil recovery. This assumption is belied by the production decline in fields throughout the world, such as Exxon's Prudhoe Bay, which continues to decline despite advanced recovery techniques.

Most important, the energy data on which these projections rely are often dated, highly speculative, and outright misleading. Demand estimates take years to verify. Of the world's proven reserves, 95 percent are "un-audited." There are virtually no field-by-field production reports, and supply data are imprecise and rarely objective. "See-no-evil" projections not only disguise the impending oil supply crisis, but they may contribute to its potentially catastrophic effects by keeping policymakers in the dark.

Oil Reserves and Consumption

Locations of reserves	Reserves billions of barrels
Total world, according to Dept. of Energy in 2000	2000–3000
Consumed to date	1000
Middle East	770
Venezuela	78
Former Soviet Union	76
North America	44
Nigeria	25
China	18
Annual consumption	
World	30
United States	7
U.S. imports	
1980	49%
1990	57%
2005	>70%

TAKEN FROM: Bhakta B. Rath and James M. Marder, "Powering the Future: Does the Fuel Gage Read Empty?" *Advanced Materials & Processes*, January 2007.

There is evidence to suggest that the peak is imminent, if it has not already arrived. Non-OPEC supplies are clearly nearing a peak, with five years of negligible one-to-two percent growth. Projections by the Association for the Study of Peak Oil and Gas, taking into account rising rates of decline in production growth and lower quality new oil, project the peak in 2008. But confronted with unreliable statistical projections, the best way to make an educated guess about peaking oil supply may simply be to observe where oil comes from. With increasing water incursion into reserves, serious problems with corrosion, and high risks associated with efforts to increase production, the world's most important oil production sites are simply in increasingly poor shape.

Terrorism and Instability in Oil Regions

Demand outpacing supply is not the world's only energy dilemma. The safety and security of energy infrastructure raises a host of issues. The list of "flash points" where some dreadful event could suddenly affect energy supply grows every day. When terrorists attempted to attack Saudi Arabia's Abqaiq oil processing plant, it justifiably sent shivers up energy observers' spines. This massive complex, guarded by a series of chain-link fences, processes every barrel of light and extra light Saudi crude. Had the attack been successful, the world could suddenly have been without more than 6 million barrels per day of high quality oil for an extended period.

The narrow and shallow Straits of Malacca are a conduit for almost 11 million barrels a day of Middle East Oil streaming to Singapore, China, Taiwan, Japan, and Korea. Terrorist attacks on only a handful of large crude oil tankers could shut off Asia's oil for what could also be a very long time.

Re-emergence of civil strife in Nigeria's oil-bearing Niger Delta, Venezuelan President Hugo Chavez's constant threats to cease selling Venezuelan oil to the United States, and threats by Ecuador and Peru to nationalize their oil resources—recently acted upon by the former country—all constitute risks to the steady flow of global oil.

Had the global oil and gas system maintained a significant cushion of spare productive capacity, the energy system could tolerate one or two of these unforeseen events. But that spare capacity was used up by steadily rising demand. Today, virtually all oil and gas fields produce at the highest rates they can sustain. The tanker fleet, the global drilling fleet, the world's high quality complex refineries are all at full capacity. Adding capacity to any of these will take years.

Poor Maintenance Slows Production

A final and more subtle energy risk receiving almost no attention is that most of our global energy infrastructure is silently rusting away. A high percentage of the world's key pipelines are well beyond their original design life. Many tankers and offshore drilling rigs are too old and were not maintained during the long period when oil prices were so low that few producers made any money. Experts now speculate that more than 25 percent of the world's offshore jack-up rigs are essentially technically obsolete. This summer, we suddenly discovered that the United States' largest and one of its newer major oil fields, Prudhoe Bay, suffers serious corrosion problems, as do many North Sea oil platforms.

The world is now out of spare capacity of oil and gas at the wellhead. The world is also out of spare drilling rigs. Almost all of the world's key refineries operate at full capacity until their owners scramble to perform minimum refinery maintenance. The energy industry's workforce, from senior executives to blue collar oilfield workers, is graying. The oilfield depression lasted too long. Too many energy companies spent the last decade making sure they could survive a low-price environment and laid off too many skilled workers and hired no replacements. This lack of personnel will haunt the energy industry for the next decade or two. This deficit of human capital makes rig and refinery shortages even more complex.

Predicting Future Crisis

The oil and gas system is far too tight, with only tiny cushions to offset an accident, more corrosion problems, an earthquake, a hurricane or a terrorist attack on any of a long list of vulnerable sites. When the world last had two oil shortages in 1973 and 1979, both were traumatic to the global economy. But they were easy to fix, as neither represented a permanent problem or a shortage lasting several years.

If a major accident happened to any of our petroleum highways, ranging from the Suez Canal or the Panama Canal to far more dangerous flash points like the Straits of Malacca, it would only take a matter of weeks before all usable crude and finished product inventories were used up and shortages began to shut down key parts of the global economy. If shortages trigger hoarding, the world's stores could soon be empty and its roads traffic-free. Only energy has the potential to shut down the entire world.

There is no way to completely prevent events that shut off key supply points. But the worse and more lasting problem would be for steadily growing oil demand to silently slide ahead of useable supply, creating a shortage with no easy fix. There is no way to deal with this issue other than the difficult process of reducing demand, but it may pose the gravest risk to the sustainability of today's global economy.

While many optimistic energy observers still argue that doomsayers or pessimists are wrong, the issue is now sufficiently serious that the optimists need to introduce more than tired phrases to the debate. If rosy projections turn out to be misguided—and over the past decade, none of the optimists' vocal arguments has borne out—the impending energy supply crisis could become one of the ugliest global tipping points that our economy has ever experienced.

> "As the [oil] industry improves its ability to draw new life from old wells and expands its forays into ever-deeper corners of the globe, it is providing a strong rebuttal in the long-running debate over when the world might run out of oil."

Global Oil Reserves Are Not Near Depletion

Jad Mouawad

Jad Mouawad is a reporter for the New York Times, *covering energy issues and global politics. In this viewpoint, Mouawad states that oil companies are investing in and utilizing better technologies to extract oil resources. Some of these innovations are used to recover hard-to-get oil from existing fields; others are employed to locate new, untapped oil beds. Mouawad suggests that fears of a peak in the world's oil supplies are unfounded because doomsayers are not taking into account the industry's resourcefulness and have simply underestimated the amount of usable oil locked within the earth.*

As you read, consider the following questions:

1. What new technologies is Chevron using to extract more oil from the fields at Bakersfield, California, according to Mouawad?

2. In Nansen G. Saleri's estimates, how many barrels of oil are still producible from the fields in Saudi Arabia?

3. By what percent does the Energy Information Administration expect global oil demand to rise in 2030, as reported by Mouawad?

BAKERSFIELD, Calif.—The Kern River oil field, discovered in 1899, was revived when Chevron engineers here started injecting high-pressured steam to pump out more oil. The field, whose production had slumped to 10,000 barrels a day in the 1960s, now [in 2007] has a daily output of 85,000 barrels.

In Indonesia, Chevron has applied the same technology to the giant Duri oil field, discovered in 1941, boosting production there to more than 200,000 barrels a day, up from 65,000 barrels in the mid-1980s.

And in Texas, Exxon Mobil expects to double the amount of oil it extracts from its Means field, which dates back to the 1930s. Exxon, like Chevron, will use three-dimensional imaging of the underground field and the injection of a gas—in this case, carbon dioxide—to flush out the oil.

Within the last decade, technology advances have made it possible to unlock more oil from old fields, and, at the same time, higher oil prices have made it economical for companies to go after reserves that are harder to reach. With plenty of oil still left in familiar locations, forecasts that the world's reserves are drying out have given way to predictions that more oil can be found than ever before.

In a wide-ranging study published in 2000, the U.S. Geological Survey estimated that ultimately recoverable resources of conventional oil totaled about 3.3 trillion barrels, of which a third has already been produced. More recently, Cambridge Energy Research Associates, an energy consultant, estimated that the total base of recoverable oil was 4.8 trillion barrels. That higher estimate—which Cambridge Energy says is likely to grow—reflects how new technology can tap into more resources.

"It's the fifth time to my count that we've gone through a period when it seemed the end of oil was near and people were talking about the exhaustion of resources," said Daniel Yergin, the chairman of Cambridge Energy and author of a Pulitzer Prize–winning history of oil, who cited similar concerns in the 1880s, after both world wars and in the 1970s. "Back then we were going to fly off the oil mountain. Instead we had a boom and oil went to $10 instead of $100."

There is still a minority view, held largely by a small band of retired petroleum geologists and some members of Congress, that oil production has peaked, but the theory has been fading. Equally contentious for the oil companies is the growing voice of environmentalists, who do not think that pumping and consuming an ever-increasing amount of fossil fuel is in any way desirable.

Increased projections for how much oil is extractable may become a political topic on many different fronts and in unpredictable ways. By reassuring the public that supplies will meet future demands, oil companies may also find legislators more reluctant to consider opening Alaska and other areas to new exploration.

On a global level, the Organization of the Petroleum Exporting Countries, which has coalesced around a price of $50 a barrel for oil, will likely see its clout reinforced in coming years. The 12-country cartel, which added Angola as its newest member this year, is poised to control more than 50 percent of the oil market in coming years, up from 35 percent today, as Western oil production declines.

Oil companies say they can provide enough supplies—which might eventually lead to lower oil and gasoline prices—but that they see few alternatives to fossil fuels. Inevitably, this means that global carbon emissions used in the transportation sector will continue to increase, and so will their contribution to global warming.

The oil industry is well known for seeking out new sources of fossil fuel in far-flung places, from the icy plains of Siberia to the deep waters off West Africa. But now the quest for new discoveries is taking place alongside a much less exotic search that is crucial to the world's energy supplies. Oil companies are returning to old or mature fields partly because there are few virgin places left to explore, and, of those, few are open to investors.

At Bakersfield, for example, Chevron is using steam-flooding technology and computerized three-dimensional models to boost the output of the field's heavy oil reserves. Even after a century of production, engineers say there is plenty of oil left to be pumped from Kern River.

"We're still finding new opportunities here," said Steve Garrett, a geophysicist with Chevron. "It's not over until you abandon the last well, and even then it's not over."

Some forecasters, studying data on how much oil is used each year and how much is still believed to be in the ground, have argued that at some point by 2010, global oil production will peak—if it has not already—and begin to fall. That drop would usher in an uncertain era of shortages, price spikes and economic decline.

"I am very, very seriously worried about the future we are facing," said Kjell Aleklett, the president of the Association for the Study of Peak Oil and Gas. "It is clear that oil is in limited supplies."

Many oil executives say that these so-called peak-oil theorists fail to take into account the way that sophisticated technology, combined with higher prices that make searches for new oil more affordable, are opening up opportunities to develop supplies. As the industry improves its ability to draw new life from old wells and expands its forays into ever-deeper corners of the globe, it is providing a strong rebuttal in the long-running debate over when the world might run out of oil.

Typically, oil companies can only produce one barrel for every three they find. Two usually are left behind, either because they are too hard to pump out or because it would be too expensive to do so. Going after these neglected resources, energy experts say, represents a tremendous opportunity.

"Ironically, most of the oil we will discover is from oil we've already found," said Lawrence Goldstein, an energy analyst at the Energy Policy Research Foundation, an industry-funded group. "What has been missing is the technology and the threshold price that will lead to a revolution in lifting that oil."

Nansen G. Saleri, the head of reservoir management at the state-owned Saudi Aramco, said that new seismic tools giving geologists a better view of oil fields, real-time imaging software and the ability to drill horizontal wells could boost global reserves.

Mr. Saleri said that Saudi Arabia's total reserves were almost three times higher that the kingdom's officially published figure of 260 billion barrels, or about a quarter of the world's proven total.

He estimated the kingdom's resources at 716 billion barrels, including oil that has already been produced as well as more uncertain reserves. And thanks to more sophisticated technology, Mr. Saleri said he "wouldn't be surprised" if ultimate reserves in Saudi Arabia eventually reached 1 trillion barrels.

Even if the Saudi estimates are impossible to verify, they underline the fact that oil companies are constantly looking for new ways to unlock more oil from the ground.

Enough Oil for the Next Century

In 1920, the United States Geological Survey officially estimated that the U.S. had just 6.7 billion barrels of oil left, including undiscovered oil fields. Eighty-two years later, the U.S. had produced 180 billion barrels of oil and still had 22 billion barrels of proven reserves. The USGS's 1920 estimate was off by a mere 2900%.

People have long feared running out of oil, but doomsayers' predictions have all proven false. Given that there is a fixed amount of oil in the world, someday we will doubtless see prices rise due to disappearing supplies. But that hasn't happened yet, and probably won't happen for at least 30–100 years.

Virtually all fluctuations in gasoline prices have been due to political events and natural disasters, not to actual shortages of oil in the ground. Though Katrina and Rita have driven oil prices today to $65 a barrel, this is less, after adjusting for inflation, than prices in 1979–1981.

Randal O'Toole, "The Myth of Peak Oil,"
Liberty, vol. 19, no. 12, December 2005.
www.libertyunbound.com/archive/2005_12/otoole-oil.html.

At the Kern River field just outside of Bakersfield, millions of gallons of steam are injected into the field to melt the oil, which has the unusually dense consistency of very thick molasses. The steamed liquid is then drained through underground reservoirs and pumped out by about 8,500 production wells scattered around the field, which covers 20 square miles.

Initially, engineers expected to recover only 10 percent of the field's oil. Now, thanks to decades of trial and error, Chevron believes it will be able to recover up to 80 percent of the oil from the field, more than twice the industry's average recovery rate, which is typically around 35 percent. Each well produces about 10 barrels a day at a cost of $16 each. That compares with production costs of only $1 or $2 a barrel in the Persian Gulf, home to the world's lowest-cost producers.

Chevron hopes to use the knowledge it has obtained from this vast open-air, and underground, laboratory and apply it to similar heavy oil fields around the world. It is also planning a large pilot program to test the technology in an area between Saudi Arabia and Kuwait, for example.

Oil companies have been perfecting so-called secondary and tertiary recovery methods—injecting all sorts of exotic gases and liquids into oil fields, including water and soap, natural gas, carbon dioxide and even hydrogen sulfide, a foul-smelling and poisonous gas.

Since the dawn of the Petroleum Age more than a century ago, the world has consumed more than 1 trillion barrels of oil. Most of that was of the light, liquid kind that was easy to find, easy to pump and easy to refine. But as these light sources are depleted, a growing share of the world's oil reserves are made out of heavier oil.

Analysts estimate there are about 1 trillion barrels of heavy oil, tar sands, and shale-oil deposits in places like Canada, Venezuela and the United States that can be turned into liquid fuel by enhanced recovery methods like steam-flooding.

"This is an industry that moves in cycles, and right now, enormous amounts of innovation, technology and investments are being unleashed," said Mr. Yergin, the author and energy consultant.

After years of underinvestment, oil companies are now in a global race to increase supplies to catch the growth of consumption. The world consumed about 31 billion barrels of oil [in 2006]. Because of population and economic growth, especially in Asian and developing countries, oil demand is forecast to rise 40 percent by 2030 to 43 billion barrels, according to the Energy Information Administration.

Back in California, the Kern River field itself seems little changed from what it must have looked like 100 years ago. The same dusty hills are now littered with a forest of wells, with gleaming pipes running along dusty roads. Seismic technology and satellites are now used to monitor operations while sensors inside the wells record slight changes in temperature or pressure. Each year, the company drills some 850 new wells there.

Amazingly, there are very few workers in the field. Engineers in air-conditioned control rooms can get an accurate picture of the field's underground reservoir and pinpoint with accuracy the areas they want to explore. None of that technology was available just a decade ago.

"Yes, there are finite resources in the ground, but you never get to that point," Jeff Hatlen, an engineer with Chevron, said on a recent tour of the field.

In 1978, when he started his career here, operators believed the field would be abandoned within 15 years. "That's why peak oil is a moving target," Mr. Hatlen said. "Oil is always a function of price and technology."

> "Many Americans see terrorism as the principal threat to security but, for much of humanity, the effects of water shortages and rising temperatures on food availability are far more important issues."

Food Scarcity Is a Global Problem

Lester R. Brown

In this viewpoint, Lester R. Brown, a noted environmentalist, states that millions of people on the planet are suffering from food scarcity. Brown predicts that because of recent temperature peaks and resulting droughts, croplands across the globe will yield weaker harvests and fresh water supplies will shrink. Such trends will not only impact major agricultural nations but also those countries that rely heavily on imported grains and other foodstuffs. Brown is the president of the Earth Policy Institute, an organization based in Washington, DC, that promotes environmental sustainability.

As you read, consider the following questions:

1. As Brown lists them, what are some of the telltale indicators that the global demand for food and water is outstripping supply and consequently damaging a sustainable environment?

2. What was the amount of grain harvest shortfall that Europe experienced after a season of high temperatures in 2003, according to Brown?

3. In Brown's view, what are the three principal steps needed to secure future food supplies?

[In late 2005], rising oil prices have focused the world's attention on the depletion of vital reserves, but the drying up of underground water resources from overpumping is a far more serious issue. Excessive pumping for irrigation to satisfy food needs today almost guarantees a decline in food production tomorrow. There are substitutes for oil; the same cannot be said for water.

The growth in population since 1950 exceeds that during the preceding 4,000,000 years. Perhaps more striking, the world economy has expanded sixfold since 1950. As the economy grows, its demands are outstripping the Earth, exceeding many of the planet's natural capacities to provide food, water, and the basic needs of daily living. Evidence of these excessive demands can be seen in collapsing fisheries, shrinking forests, expanding deserts, escalating CO_2 levels, eroding soils, elevated temperatures, disappearing species, falling water tables, melting glaciers, deteriorating grasslands, rising seas, and rivers that are running dry. Nearly all these environmental trends affect world food security.

Falling Water Tables and Rising Temperatures

Two of the newer trends—falling water tables and rising temperatures—are making it far more difficult for the world's farmers to feed the 76,000,000 people added to our numbers each year. Humans drink nearly four quarts of water a day in one form or another, but the food we consume on a daily basis requires 2,000 quarts of water to produce. Agriculture is the most water-intensive sector of the economy: 70% of all water pumped from underground or diverted from rivers is used for irrigation; 20% is employed by industry; and 10% goes to residences.

Water tables currently are falling in countries that contain over half the world's people. The vast majority of the nearly 3,000,000,000 individuals to be added to world population by mid-century will come in nations where water tables already are falling and wells are going dry. Historically, it was the supply of land that constrained the growth in food production. Today, though, the shortage of water is the most formidable barrier.

Rising temperatures are the second big threat to future food security. During the last few years, crop ecologists focusing on the precise relationship between temperature and crop yields have found that each 1°C rise in temperature during the growing season reduces the yield of grain—wheat, rice, and corn—by 10%. Since 1970, the Earth's average temperature has risen nearly 0.7°C (1°F). The five warmest years during 124 seasons of record-keeping occurred in the last seven calendar turns [i.e; since 1999].

In 2002, record high temperatures and drought lowered grain harvests in India and the U.S. These reduced harvests helped pull world grain production some 90,000,000 tons below consumption, a shortfall of more than four percent.

In 2003, it was Europe that bore the brunt of rising temperatures. The record-breaking heat wave that claimed 35,000 lives in eight countries withered grain harvests in virtually every nation from France in the west through the Ukraine in the east. The resulting reduction in Europe's grain production of some 30,000,000 tons was equal to half the U.S. wheat harvest.

Although climate change is discussed widely, we are not quick to grasp its full meaning for food security. Everyone knows that the Earth's temperature is rising, but commodity analysts often condition their projections on weather returning to "normal," failing to realize that, with climate conditions now in flux, there is no "normal" to return to.

The Intergovernmental Panel on Climate Change, a group of some 2,000 scientists, projects that the Earth's average temperature will rise during this century by 2–10°F. Young farmers face the prospect of higher temperatures than any generation of growers since agriculture began.

Higher temperatures in mountainous regions alter the precipitation mix, increasing rainfall and reducing snow accumulation. The result is more flooding during the rainy season and less snowmelt to feed rivers during the dry season. In Asia, for instance, this shift is affecting the flow of the major rivers that originate in the vast Himalayan-Tibetan region, including the Indus, Ganges, Mekong, Yangtze, and Yellow.

Decreased Harvest

The world has been sluggish in responding to these new threats. In four of the last five years [i.e., since 2001], the world grain harvest has fallen short of consumption. As a result, world grain stocks are at their lowest level in 30 years. Another large world grain shortfall [in 2006] could drop stocks to the lowest level on record and send world food prices into uncharted territory.

Among the trio of grains that dominate world food production—wheat, rice, and corn—the supply of rice is likely to tighten first simply because it is the most water-dependent of the three. Finding enough water to expand rice production is

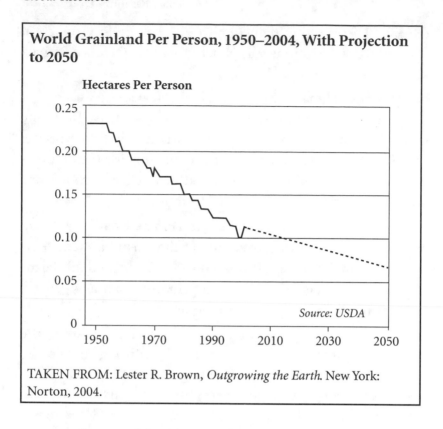

World Grainland Per Person, 1950–2004, With Projection to 2050

TAKEN FROM: Lester R. Brown, *Outgrowing the Earth.* New York: Norton, 2004.

not easy in a world with spreading water scarcity. If rice supplies shrink and prices rise, the higher costs are likely to affect wheat as well.

Perhaps the biggest agricultural reversal in recent times has been the precipitous decline in China's grain production by 50,000,000 tons between 1998 and 2004. Since 1998, China has covered this decline by drawing down its once-massive stocks, causing it to turn to the world market. Its purchase of 8,000,000 tons of wheat to import in 2004 could signal the beginning of a shift from a world food economy dominated by surpluses to one ruled by scarcity.

Overnight, China has become the world's largest wheat importer. Yet it will almost certainly import even more in the future, as well as vast quantities of rice and corn. It is this potential need to import up to 50,000,000 tons of grain annually within the next few years and the associated emergence of a politics of food scarcity that is likely to put this issue on the front pages of newspapers.

At the other end of the spectrum is Brazil, the only country with the potential to expand world cropland area markedly. However, what will the environmental consequences be of continuing to clear and plow Brazil's vast interior? Will the soils sustain cultivation over the longer term? How many plant and animal species will be sacrificed to expand its exports of soybeans?

An Opportunity for Corrective Policies

World food security is a far more complex issue today than it was a generation ago. In earlier times, if world grain supplies tightened, the U.S. simply returned some of its idled cropland to production, quickly expanding the harvest and reestablishing price stability. That commodity set-aside program was phased out in 1995, depriving the world of this ready reserve of cropland that could be brought into production quickly.

Today, food security—once the exclusive province of agricultural ministers—is far more involved. It is perhaps a commentary on the tenor of our times that decisions made in ministries of energy can have a greater effect on future food security than those reached in ministries of agriculture. Policies formulated by ministers of water resources also directly can affect food production and prices. Moreover, with irrigation water availability per person shrinking for the world as a whole, ministries of health and family planning also may have a greater affect on future food security.

The three principal steps needed to secure future food supplies are worldwide efforts to raise water productivity, cut carbon emissions, and stabilize population. If the global community does not act quickly to raise water productivity, falling tables soon could translate into rising food prices. Given the effect of higher temperatures on crop yields, the urgency of cutting carbon emissions sharply cannot easily be overstated.

The good news is that we have the technologies to do this. For example, if, over the next decade, the U.S. was to shift its entire automobile fleet to gas-electric hybrid engines with efficiencies comparable to today's Toyota Prius, the country easily could slice gasoline use in half.

On the supply side, the potential for cutting coal use and carbon emissions by developing wind resources to generate electricity has enormous potential. In Europe, which is leading the world into the wind era, and where coal mines are closing, some 40,000,000 residents receive electricity from wind farms. By 2020, half of Europe's 400,000,000 people are projected to get their residential electricity from wind.

These are but two of the hundreds of steps that can be taken to cut carbon emissions and stabilize climate. Ironically, given the role of automobiles in raising the atmospheric carbon dioxide levels that drive climate change, the fuel efficiency of the vehicle we drive to the supermarket may affect the price of the foodstuffs inside that very same store.

Many Americans see terrorism as the principal threat to security but, for much of humanity, the effects of water shortages and rising temperatures on food availability are far more important issues. For the 3,000,000,000 people who live on two dollars a day or less and who spend up to 70% of their income on food, even a modest rise in prices quickly can become life-threatening. For them, it is the next meal that is the overriding concern.

> "Over the past 35 years, the world's food
> production has expanded faster than
> its population."

Food Distribution, Not Scarcity, Is a Global Problem

Roger Thurow and Jay Solomon

Roger Thurow and Jay Solomon contend in this viewpoint that the world produces enough food to feed all people, but the distribution mechanisms are not in place to ensure that food can be delivered to those who are hungry. Using India as an example, the authors describe how one part of the solution to this problem is to raise standards of living in developing nations. India is investing in road building and local economies to get food to the nation's rural poor and to give them the power to purchase it. Thurow and Solomon suggest that this type of response has helped some Indians overcome persistent hunger but would have to be greatly expanded and earn the cooperation of governments to make a dent in the problem of global hunger. Currently based in Europe, Roger Thurow is a senior writer for the Wall Street Journal. *Jay Solomon is a staff writer for the same newspaper.*

Roger Thurow and Jay Solomon, "An Indian Paradox: Bumper Harvests and Rising Hunger," *Wall Street Journal*, June 25, 2004, p. A1. Copyright © 2004 The New York Times Company. Republished with permission of *Wall Street Journal*, conveyed through Copyright Clearance Center, Inc.

As you read, consider the following questions:

1. According to the United Nations, how many calories per day could the world's farmers provide to each person on the planet in 2002?

2. As Thurow and Solomon report, why did India's large grain stocks never reach its 214 million hungry citizens?

3. Why did India choose to export much of its grain in 2001 instead of retaining it for future use?

THIRUKANCHIPET, India—In the 1960s, this country set out to prevent famine by boosting agricultural production. The push was so successful that wheat and rice stockpiles approached 60 million tons. By 2001, India had its own grain export business. But Murugesan Manangatti, a 29-year-old illiterate peasant, was still hungry. He had no land to grow crops and no steady income to buy food.

Last summer, an agricultural research foundation gave Mr. Manangatti some unusual advice: Drive a taxi. With the foundation's help, he and 15 members of this rural village received a loan to buy a three-wheeled, battery-powered vehicle. The taxi business earns up to $25 a day and Mr. Manangatti takes home a monthly salary of about $55. For the first time, he says, his family is regularly able to eat three nutritious meals a day.

The Thirukanchipet taxi is a fresh approach to solving a jarring paradox. The world is producing more food than ever before as countries such as India, China and Brazil emerge as forces in global agriculture. But at the same time, the number of the world's hungry is on the rise—including in India—after falling for decades. Despite its overflowing granaries, India has more hungry people than any other country, as many as 214 million according to United Nations estimates, or one-fifth of its population.

More Money, More Food

The paradox is propelling a shift in strategy among the world's hunger fighters. International agencies that once encouraged countries to solve starvation crises by growing more food are now tackling the more fundamental problem of rural poverty as well. The old development mantra—produce more food, feed more people—is giving way to a new call: Create more jobs, provide income to buy food.

"Increasing production is great, but we have to think about the whole chain," says M.S. Swaminathan, the 78-year-old scientist who helped engineer India's agriculture boom and whose foundation set up Mr. Manangatti's taxi. India has been able to conquer its famine of food, he says. Now it is suffering from a "famine of jobs and livelihoods."

The stark contrast between food production and rural poverty is helping to transform Indian politics. India's ruling Bharatiya Janata Party [BJP] had overseen a boom in the country's technology sector but was defeated in May [2004] elections largely by the votes of a rural population that felt left behind. The BJP's "India Shining" campaign, which highlighted the country's economic advances, was trumped by the victorious Congress party, which ran on a platform of aiding farmers.

There is plenty of supply on hand to meet global demand. Over the past 35 years, the world's food production has expanded faster than its population. In 2002, according to the United Nations World Food Program [WFP], farmers produced enough food to provide every person with 2,800 calories a day. That's equivalent to the general daily requirement of teen boys and active men, according to the U.S. government's dietary guidelines. The WFP's feeding programs aim to provide 2,100 calories a day to their recipients.

But inadequate infrastructure, local corruption and rural poverty have prevented the chronically hungry—those who don't eat enough to fulfill basic standards—from gaining access to this bountiful harvest. After falling for decades, the estimated number of undernourished in the developing world increased by 18 million to 798 million between 1997 and 2001, according to the latest data from the U.N.'s Food and Agriculture Organization.

Failures in the Chain of Distribution

In a typical year, the World Food Program distributes food to about 90 million people, many of whom are threatened with starvation in disaster situations such as drought. Most of the remaining 700 million live on isolated, stingy land, and have neither the money to buy food nor the ability to grow it. They're beyond the reach of international feeding programs and also fall through national safety nets.

It's virtually impossible to simply hand out food surpluses to the hungry because of the cost and complexity of distribution. It would also turn recipients into permanent wards of the world. "I believe in [Mohandis K.] Gandhi's strategy: Don't turn people into beggars," says Mr. Swaminathan.

Looking for solutions, countries are turning their attention to permanent development projects such as road building that can foster economic activity for the rural poor and connect them to markets for their produce.

A [2004] summit meeting of the Group of Eight industrialized nations embraced a plan to "end the cycle of famine" in the Horn of Africa. One plan for Ethiopia involves creating work programs that would allow the five million people there dependent on aid to buy their own food. Earlier [in 2004], the Chinese government said it would cut farming taxes and boost investment in rural areas. And at a [2004] meeting of the African Union, leaders committed to allocating at least 10% of their budgets to agriculture and rural development.

The WFP, in one strategy shift, is emphasizing schools with a classroom-based feeding program that so far reaches 15 million. It's designed to encourage children, who constitute about 300 million of the world's hungry, to attend school and at the same time combat malnutrition. "An ill-educated, unhealthy population can't take advantage of an open economy," says John Powell, a WFP deputy executive director.

Good Grain Harvests

India's agricultural program of the 1960s, dubbed the Green Revolution, was launched after the country suffered through a series of famines. Under the guidance of local and international agronomists and scientists, Indian farmers were introduced to hardy, fast-growing wheat strains and better uses of fertilizer and irrigation. As a result, crop yields multiplied, and in recent years India's wheat production topped 70 million tons, surpassing that of the U.S. The Indian government estimates that wheat output may pass 100 million tons in the coming decade.

In the country's northern grain belt, wheat grows almost everywhere there is a level field, between houses and schools, and brick factories and gas stations. During the harvest season, the roads are clogged with tractors such as the small Massey Ferguson model driven by 19-year-old farmer Gopal Kumar. He recently pulled a wagon piled with five tons of wheat as he made his way to the mill in Mathura, a 30-minute drive from the Taj Mahal.

The Kumars have been farming wheat for three generations and now work 36 acres. "This is a pretty good year," said Mr. Kumar. He maneuvered his tractor and wagon past Mathura's McDonald's and delivered his wheat to Rajender Bansal's mill. Mr. Bansal opened his mill about 10 years ago with capacity to process 2,000 tons of wheat a month. He has since expanded to 3,000 tons.

As India's grain production grew, so did its surpluses. By 2001, the national stockpile of rice and wheat was approaching 60 million tons, according to the government. The country had also become one of the world's leading producers of

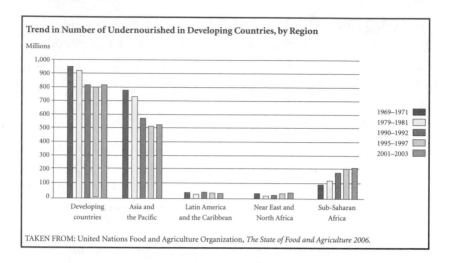

Trend in Number of Undernourished in Developing Countries, by Region

TAKEN FROM: United Nations Food and Agriculture Organization, *The State of Food and Agriculture 2006*.

fruits, vegetables and milk. India set up a distribution network to supply surplus grain at reduced prices to 180 million families.

Mismanaged Distribution

But with inefficiency and local mismanagement plaguing distribution, it couldn't move the grain fast enough through the system. Some even spoiled in warehouses. A 2002 government survey concluded that 48% of children under five years old are malnourished. That's an improvement from three decades ago and even today, given rapid population growth, the proportion of chronically hungry Indians continues to fall. But in a sign that there are limits to the Green Revolution, the absolute number of hungry people in India began to rise again in the late 1990s, according to the U.N.

With the cost of storing surpluses spiraling, the government opened the door to grain exports in 2001. India sold more than 10 million tons of grain to overseas customers that year, mostly in Asia and the Middle East.

Traders from traditional wheat and rice exporters were critical of the Indian trade. How could the country export grain while so many in the country are hungry? D. P. Singh, chairman of the All India Grain Exporters Association, says the grain surplus has been big enough to allow for both exporting and distribution to the rural poor. "If [the grain] didn't reach the hungry people, it's too bad, but it has nothing to do with availability," he says.

Persistent Hunger

At the same time, India made a donation of one million tons of wheat to a World Food Program project in Afghanistan. A few European members of the WFP's executive board questioned the propriety of India's action. Himachal Som, India's representative to the U.N.'s food agencies in Rome, made an impassioned speech to his critics arguing that the donation didn't affect the country's ability to feed its poor, a more intractable problem than simply growing greater amounts of food.

The results of [the May 2004] election in India are concentrating attention on the paradox of hunger. In the two states where the former BJP-led government fared especially badly—Andhra Pradesh and Tamil Nadu—the gap between India's high-tech centers and surrounding farming areas had become the most pronounced. Hyderabad, the capital of Andhra Pradesh, grew prosperous as the state's government courted U.S. companies such as Microsoft Corp. and General Electric Co., and the World Bank praised the state for its economic progress.

But about 100 miles outside the city's glittering office towers, farmers in the town of Kalimela say they've benefited little. A three-year drought hit farm production. Many blamed the state government for failing to invest more in irrigation systems and roads. In addition, farmers were hit hard when the state increased electricity rates.

"The government hasn't helped us. No roads. No water. Right from the beginning," says Jarappa Sonia, 35, a sugarcane and wheat farmer from Kalimela. Mr. Sonia joined a government work program building roads in a district four hours from his home. "I prefer to be a farmer," he says.

The opposition Congress party promised free power for Andhra Pradesh's farmers. Within hours of taking office, the state's new chief minister, Y. S. Rajasekhar Reddy, honored that pledge.

It's too early to know how fully the Congress-led government will implement its ideas. The Congress party and its allies have agreed to support minimum-wage public-works programs such as a guaranteed 100 days of employment for rural households. They have also promised to improve farmers' access to credit and restructure outstanding debts.

Increasing Income to End Hunger

Providing rural folk with an income to buy food is a theory the Swaminathan foundation has extended to 9,600 people in 800 self-help groups in five states across the country.

In the small southern village of Thirukanchipet, the best the rural unemployed can hope for is seasonal work in rice paddies for $1 or $2 a day. Earlier this year, with the help of the Swaminathan foundation, 28 men and women formed a dairy group to improve their credit worthiness and received a micro-credit loan of about $10,000 from a local bank.

The group bought 20 cows and 19 calves, and built a milking shed. The cows produce more than 40 gallons a day, which is sold to a local dairy cooperative for 80 cents a gallon. Much of the daily income of about $30 is set aside to repay the loan. The rest is distributed among the members who for the first time are able to afford the higher-quality rice and wheat sold in the private stores instead of that in government ration shops.

"It tastes better," says M. Kanagaraj, a tall, thin man of 34. He is one of four workers who milk and manage the cows and makes about $40 a month. "We eat two meals a day now," he says. They are waiting for the calves to mature, so they can double the milk production and their income.

"Then," says Mr. Kanagaraj, "we will eat three meals a day."

> "*Tensions exist over water use, water ownership and water rights—and are likely to increase in the future.*"

Water Scarcity Is a Global Problem

Steve Lonergan

Steve Lonergan is a divisional director at the United Nations Environment Programme. He is also the co-author, with David Brooks, of Watershed: The Role of Freshwater in the Israeli-Palestinian Conflict. *In this viewpoint, Lonergan asserts that water is a scarce resource in some parts of the world and that access to freshwater reserves is an international concern that has heightened regional tensions. He maintains that water rights and water disputes are issues that will continue to shape international policies, but that these matters are not likely to lead to open hostilities. Lonergan argues that cleaner water supplies and the efficient transport of water must be assured before their lack unnecessarily adds to regional problems.*

As you read, consider the following questions:

1. In what part of the world is water a "strategic" resource, as Lonergan explains?

Steve Lonergan, "Water and War," *Our Planet*, 2005. Reproduced by permission.

2. In what sector of the global economy does Lonergan believe the most improvement in the efficient use of water can be made?

3. In Lonergan's view, what two things will be needed to avert future problems over water rights and supply?

The purposes of the United Nations, as set forth in the UN Charter, are to maintain international peace and security; to develop friendly relations among nations; to cooperate in solving international economic, social, cultural and humanitarian problems and in promoting respect for human rights and fundamental freedoms; and to be a centre for harmonizing the actions of nations in attaining these ends. These purposes were reinforced in the United Nations Millennium Declaration of 2000 and further clarified. Three key areas now define United Nations activities: Peace and Security; Development; and Human Rights and Democracy.

As we enter the 21st century, new challenges to these areas are emerging. We are confronted with both old and new threats to international peace and security; poverty has been recognized by world leaders as the most daunting of all the problems facing the world in the new century; and fundamental values of freedom, equality, solidarity, tolerance, respect for nature and shared responsibility now form common values through which achievements in the former two categories can be realized. In each of these key areas environment and resources play a central role. Threats to common security now include so-called 'soft threats': environmental degradation, resource depletion, contagious diseases and corruption, to name just a few.

It is now recognized that environmental degradation and both scarcity and abundance of natural resources are potential sources of conflict—and cooperation—and need to be more systematically addressed in this context. Access to fresh water

Living Below the Water Requirement Threshold

Hydrologists typically assess scarcity by looking at the population–water equation. . . . the convention is to treat 1,700 cubic metres per person as the national threshold for meeting water requirements for agriculture, industry, energy and the environment. Availability below 1,000 cubic metres is held to represent a state of "water scarcity"—and below 500 cubic metres, "absolute scarcity".

Today, about 700 million people in 43 countries live below the water-stress threshold. With average annual availability of about 1,200 cubic metres per person the Middle East is the world's most water-stressed region: only Iraq, Iran, Lebanon and Turkey are above the threshold. Palestinians, especially in Gaza, experience some of the world's most acute water scarcity—about 320 cubic metres per person. Sub-Saharan Africa has the largest number of water-stressed countries of any region. Almost a quarter of Sub-Saharan Africa's population lives in a water-stressed country today—and that share is rising.

United Nations Development Programme,
Human Development Report 2006.
New York: Palgrave Macmillan, 2006, pp. 135–36.

and sanitation services are a precondition to achieving the other internationally accepted goals in the Millennium Declaration.

Nowhere is this issue more important than in the Middle East, where water is considered a 'strategic' resource and tensions between countries in the region over it are high. There it has become a major political issue, and the various peace agreements that have been proposed or signed in recent years all include water. This has led to claims from various sources—

attributed (but unsubstantiated) to such individuals as [former secretary-general of the UN] Boutros Boutros Ghali and former King Hussein of Jordan—that 'the next war in the Middle East will be over water'. This rhetoric has captured the public imagination and caused much consternation in the intelligence communities of various countries, who worry whether water—or other scarce resources—may be a future flashpoint for international conflict.

Scarce Resource

In many cases, these comments are little more than media hype; in others, statements have been made for political reasons. Yet, regardless of the source, or the reason, water is clearly a scarce resource in some regions. Tensions exist over water use, water ownership and water rights—and are likely to increase in the future. The Middle East and Africa provoke perhaps the greatest concern about water shortage: by 2025, 40 countries in the regions are expected to experience water stress or scarcity.

Water scarcity is a function of supply and demand. Demand is increasing at an alarming rate in some regions, through population growth and increasing per capita use. In many water-scarce countries, such as Jordan and Israel, there is no obvious and inexpensive way to increase water supply, and tensions among different water users are likely to result. In other countries, such as Egypt, improvements in water efficiency, moving away from water-intensive crops, or importing water from nearby countries may offer reasonable solutions.

The second crisis is deteriorating water quality. Agriculture is the biggest polluter: increased use of fertilizer and pesticides has contaminated both groundwater and surface water supplies. Domestic and industrial pollution is also increasing, and the problem affects both developed and developing countries.

Finally, the use of water has a geopolitical dimension. Water moves from upstream to downstream users, and withdrawals and type of use in one place may affect the quantity or quality of supplies downstream. There are also historical, cultural, economic and social aspects of water use. To some, water is a gift from God, and should not be priced, while others, such as the World Bank, have pushed for full marginal cost pricing of water.

The lack of a suitable legal framework for resolving international water resource disputes presents another problem. Sovereignty over international rivers generally invokes one of four doctrines: absolute territorial sovereignty, which implies that riparian states [countries abutting water sources] may use water resources in any way they please, even to the detriment of other nations; absolute territorial integrity, which suggests that riparian use of a river should not negatively affect downstream riparians; limited territorial sovereignty, which invokes a combination of the two within a framework of equitable use by all parties; and community of co-riparian states, which promotes integrated management of river basins.

Global Implications

Problems of water scarcity and water pollution affect human and ecosystem health, and hinder economic and agricultural development. Local and regional problems, in turn, may affect the rest of the world by threatening food supplies and global economic development. The United Nations Commission on Sustainable Development concludes that these problems could result in a series of local and regional water crises, with serious global implications.

Is there likely to be violent conflict over water in the future? Past experience suggests that this is unlikely. However, many claim that the probability of conflict is increasing. The basis for most projections for future conflicts is that with the growth of demand, the decline in freshwater availability (through groundwater mining and pollution), and the adverse health effects from poor water quality, scarcity will result in violence and water wars. Yet fighting over water makes very little sense economically or politically.

There is little question that water scarcity will be a problem in some regions in the future. Global warming is likely to alter rainfall patterns and evapo-transpiration regimes in many regions, and long-term planning for water supply must take this into consideration. There is also little question that water will cost more, as it becomes increasingly scarce. This will necessitate improvements in water efficiency—and possibly the restructuring of economies away from water-intensive sectors.

The greatest improvements can be made in agriculture, since irrigation here accounts for almost 70 per cent of water use worldwide. As the price of water increases, different distribution systems are coming into operation: water moved by tanker, by long-distance pipeline and even by plastic bags. There may also be greater use of desalination technology, although to date it has been prohibitively expensive and operations are confined primarily to countries with surplus energy supplies. Importing water—as in Singapore—may become more normal.

Two other factors may play a role in water-related tension. First, food imports may be driven by water scarcity. Half the world population will soon depend on the world food market for their food security. How poor, water-scarce countries will finance these food imports may become a major issue. Second, increased competition is expected for water: between urban and rural populations; between the agriculture and domestic sectors; and between countries. This may be exacerbated by rapid urbanization. Nevertheless many of the problems with water supply in the future can be resolved thrugh cooperative agreements and some degree of economic investment. Such agreements and preventative diplomacy over shared water supplies will continue to dominate.

Disputes Over Water

Historically, there is little evidence that water scarcity has caused violent conflict though, in many cases, water has been used as a strategic goal or target, as part of military activities. There have, however, been many disputes over water within nations: it may be that the probability of violent conflict over water varies inversely with the size (and type) of the political bodies involved.

Yet water scarcity will be at the forefront of the international agenda for decades to come. In some cases, water may even be a contributing factor in international conflict. A member of the Israeli negotiating team to the Middle East Peace Process, Hydrology Professor Uri Shamir once noted: "If there is a political will for peace, water will not be a hindrance. If you want reasons to fight, water will give you ample opportunities."

"Unlike oil, water is a reusable resource, which can be used and then reused many times."

Water Scarcity Is Not a Global Problem

Asit K. Biswas

In this viewpoint, Asit K. Biswas counters notions that water is becoming a scarce global resource. Biswas states that current predictions of future water requirements (for industry, agriculture, and personal use) are overestimated because they rely on present-day methods of management, which have unfortunately led to widespread waste. As time progresses, Biswas argues, more efficient water management, utilization, and recovery are being incorporated throughout the globe, and these practices will ensure that water remains a reusable resource. In addition, Biswas believes that the amount of water available for use is also underestimated, giving the false impression that water is already a scarce resource. Asit K. Biswas is the president of the Third World Centre for Water Management, a research think tank in Mexico. He is also the author of over 50 books, many of which concern water resources.

Asit K. Biswas, "An Assessment of Future Global Water Issues," *International Journal of Water Resources Development*, vol. 21, no. 2, June 2005, pp. 229–37.

As you read, consider the following questions:

1. As some scientists estimate, about how many times is each drop of water in the Colorado River used before it reaches the sea?

2. According to Biswas, what will eventually drive nations to explore and tap the currently-neglected groundwater resources of the planet?

3. In Biswas's view, what two factors might induce a global water crisis if they are not promptly addressed?

While predicting the future is an extremely hazardous business, one item can be predicted with complete certainty: the world in the year 2030 will be vastly different from what it is today. The changes that we shall witness during the next 25 years are likely to be far-ranging and far-reaching, and these changes will certainly be several orders of magnitude higher and more complex than what we have witnessed during the past 25 years. Among the main driving forces that are likely to contribute to these changes are rapidly evolving demographic conditions, concurrent urbanization and ruralization in developing countries, rapid technological advances, the speed, extent and impacts of globalization, improvements in human capital, governance and functioning of institutions, implementation of more effective national and intergovernmental policies, and advances in human expectations and knowledge due to accelerating information and the communications revolution.

The water sector is an integral component of the global system, and it will most certainly undergo major changes during the next 25 years. In fact, *water management practices and processes are likely to experience more change during the next 25 years than has occurred during the past 2000 years.* Many of these new developments will be driven by changes stemming from non-water sectors, on which the water profession will have no, or at best limited, control or say.

Customarily, water professionals have mostly ignored the global forces that are external to the water sector, even though these are likely to shape water use, availability and management practices of the future in some very significant ways. For example, water professionals are continuing to ignore the implications of globalization, even though within the next 5–15 years the various forces unleashed by globalization are likely to make radical changes in water use and requirement patterns in numerous countries, ranging from the United States to Japan, and China to Mexico. These types of global forces are already shaping the future use and availability patterns for water, and yet such issues have been consistently ignored by the water and development professions, and international and national institutions in the recent past. In addition, the water profession continues to ignore major developments in the areas of biotechnology, desalination, information and communication, etc., even though developments in these areas may influence the water futures of the world.

Fears of Scarcity

It is now widely predicted and believed that the world will face a major water crisis in the coming decades because of increasing water scarcities in numerous countries. Many international organizations, ranging from intergovernmental institutions such as the World Bank and the various United Nations agencies, to non-governmental organizations such as the World Water Council, have published world maps in recent years, all somewhat similar, which show more and more countries of the world will become water-stressed by 2050 because of increasing scarcities.

Such a 'bandwagon' effect in global thinking is of course not an exclusive issue for the water sector alone: it is prevalent in other areas. Regrettably, political correctness and bandwagons receive more attention than solid scientific studies and logical analyses. Accordingly, an important question arises as to how reliable are these predictions of an impending water crisis, even though numerous major institutions have produced very similar forecasts, often without any reference to the initial source.

An objective review of the facts on which the original forecast was based will indicate that its reliability is highly likely to be poor for a variety of reasons, only a few of which will be discussed here.

First, the data and the information on which such forecasts and maps are based are highly unreliable. Extensive analyses by the Third World Centre for Water Management indicate that the national estimates on which the current global figures are based are often erroneous (in some cases very significantly, and in others, they are totally wrong). For many major countries, such as India and China, estimates of water availability and use are currently available, but no one has a clear idea about the accuracy, relevance and usefulness of such national statistics, and the purposes for which they can be successfully used. Thus, it is impossible to get any reasonably reliable picture of the global and/or regional water situations, which are based on the aggregation of such incomplete and unreliable national data sets.

Secondly, water abstraction [removal of water from a water source] is at present widely used as a proxy for water use for such forecasts. Methodologically, this, of course, is fundamentally incorrect. Unlike oil, water is a reusable resource, which can be used and then reused many times. For example, some scientists have estimated that each drop of the Colorado River water is currently used six to seven times before it reaches the sea. Also, globally, water is being increasingly reused, both formally and informally, and all the indications are that the extent of reuse in all countries will accelerate further in the coming decades. Accordingly, the current practice of using water abstraction as a proxy for water available is already significantly erroneous, and so are the forecasts of the future based on such analyses. In about a decade, when water reuse becomes even more extensive, the practice of using water abstraction data in such a fashion will be completely meaningless because of very serious underestimation of the quantity of water that will actually be used. Thus, projecting water availability on this basis to 2050, and then predicting a global crisis, is not a meaningful exercise or good science.

Currently, no reasonable estimates exist on the extent of reuse of water, even at the national levels, let alone for the world as a whole. Some data on water reuse do exist for a very few developed countries such as Japan. In addition, the water profession, regrettably, has not considered reuse as an important factor in global water availability and use considerations, as a result of which the existing forecasts of the magnitudes of future water scarcities are highly suspect, and often somewhat meaningless.

The Impact of Economy and Technology on Recovering Water Resources

Thirdly, water pricing is likely to play an increasingly important role as the 21st century progresses. The net result of this development is likely to be significant advances in demand management, which currently plays a minor role in most countries of the world, especially for agricultural water use. This would mean that within a short period of about a decade or so, present projections of future water requirements would have to be revised downwards, most likely quite significantly because of increasing emphasis on demand management and cost recovery. Implementation of the European Framework Directive on water within the next decade is likely to further accelerate the global trend to use water pricing as an important instrument for water management.

Fourthly, as water pricing becomes more widespread, and as technology advances further, it is highly likely that the estimates of groundwater availability may have to be revised significantly upwards. At present, since water for agriculture, which is the major user of water, in most countries is virtually free and municipal water use is often highly subsidized, no economic incentive exists to explore groundwater on a comprehensive basis. Accordingly, the current global and national estimates of usable groundwater are likely to prove to be very serious underestimates. Under these conditions, the global estimates of economically usable groundwater are likely to increase significantly in the future. Due to technological advances, currently unusable sources of groundwater are likely to be used in the coming years.

Better Water Management

Furthermore, all the current estimates of the future global water requirements are likely to prove far too high, especially as demand management comes to widespread use, and reuse of water receives priority attention. These estimates will have to be revised significantly downwards during the next decade. This, of course, has also been the historical pattern. For example, all forecasts of future global water use made during the past 50 years have proved to be very serious overestimates. This trend of overestimating future water requirements is still continuing.

Simultaneously, the amount of water that is available for use at present is seriously underestimated because reuse and recycling are ignored; estimates of groundwater availability will have to be revised upwards; and technological advances are making costs of desalination and other non-conventional sources of water more and more attractive. For example, within the past five years, the cost of desalination of sea water has come down to about US$0.45 per cubic metre due to technological advances and improved management practices.

Coca-Cola Proclaims a Commitment to Better Water Management

Along with the communities where [Coca-Cola facilities] operate, we have a shared interest in finding effective solutions to water management. And that is at the heart of our approach to partnerships. Let me briefly share some examples.

In India, we've installed rainwater harvesting systems in twenty of our plants and in eight communities. The collected water is used for plant functions, as well as for recharging aquifers. Today, much of the total water that we use in our operations is renewed and returned to groundwater systems. And we believe we can do better. As responsible partners we will continue to increase the amount of water we return to local groundwater systems. We'll do this by supporting rainwater harvesting, drip irrigation and other local initiatives, such as helping restore traditional water storage systems that local communities use.

In Africa, many of our bottling partners are in the process of improving wastewater treatment at their facilities. Rather than just building a plant that serves the Coca-Coca bottler alone, we're collaborating with the Africa Development Bank, with USAID, and with local community stakeholders, to explore ways that—as partners—we can extend the scope of the bottler's efforts to benefit the community, to effectively leverage the human and physical capacity of our system for shared benefits.

Jeff Seabright, "Framing Solutions:
Building Partnerships," speech, Center for Strategic & International
Studies and Sandia National Laboratory,
Washington, D.C., February 9, 2005. www.csis.org.

Hence, given the upward adjustments in water availability and downward revisions in requirements, and the expected improvements in the management practices and the institutions that manage this resource, one can now be cautiously optimistic about the global water future.

This, of course, does not mean that it would be an easy process for all countries to adjust to the new realities of a rapidly changing global water scene. Most certainly, many countries are likely to find it difficult to manage the expected transformation without discontinuities because of sociopolitical constraints, institutional inertia, increasing management complexities, vested interests and current and past inefficient water management practices. However, since 'business as usual' will not be a feasible option for the future in all countries, policy makers, water professionals and water institutions, whether they like it or not, will be forced to react to the new conditions, most probably within the next 10–15 years. All these and other associated developments are likely to make the present 'gloom and doom' forecasts of a global crisis due to water scarcities somewhat unlikely in the coming decades.

The threat of a global water crisis because of physical scarcities only, as expected at present, is overstated. If there is to be a crisis in the water sector, it will probably occur due to two reasons, neither of which is receiving adequate attention at present.

The Problem of Deterioration

The first cause that could contribute to a crisis is continuous water quality deterioration. Globally, water quality is receiving inadequate attention, even though it has already become a critical issue. While global data on water quantity are poor, they are virtually non-existent for water quality. Even for major developed countries such as the United States or Japan, a clear picture of the national water quality situation currently does not exist. For developing countries and for countries in transition, ranging from Indonesia to Nigeria, and Russia to

Mexico, existing legal and institutional frameworks and networks for water quality monitoring are highly deficient, adequate expertise on water quality management simply does not exist and water quality laboratories suffer very seriously from poor quality control and quality assurance practices. Furthermore, senior policy makers in most developing countries become interested in water quality aspects primarily when there are major local crises due to political considerations, and/or media interventions. Sadly, for all practical purposes, water quality is still receiving only lip service from most senior bureaucrats and politicians in developing countries, countries in transition and the international institutions.

Not surprisingly, because of the above deficiencies, water quality problems are becoming increasingly serious in all developing countries. Accordingly, nearly all surface water bodies within and near urban-industrial centres are now highly polluted. While data on the existing groundwater quality are extremely poor, it is equally likely that groundwater is also becoming increasingly contaminated near centres of population.

In spite of poor water quality management practices, national data available in developing countries and countries in transition mostly give an erroneous picture of the existing water quality conditions. As a general rule, in these countries, the official pictures of water quality situations are mostly rosier than the current conditions warrant. These estimates are accepted at face value by international institutions, and are repeated in their reports without any comments and qualifications. This practice has given these erroneous estimates legitimacy, which is unwarranted. This, in turn, has given the world a false sense of security, which is likely to prove highly counterproductive in the future.

Recent estimates made by the Third World Centre for Water Management indicate that in spite of the official rhetoric and figures published by several international organizations, less than 10% of wastewater generated in Latin America is properly treated and disposed of in an environmentally acceptable fashion. The situation is likely to be very similar in Asia, and probably worse in Africa. Furthermore, most universities in the developing world do not provide appropriate education and training on water quality management. Accordingly, rapid capacity building in this area would be a Herculean task under the best of circumstances. In addition, currently no reasonable estimates exist as to what would be the investment needed in Latin America or Africa to improve wastewater treatment from paltry levels of less than 10% to a reasonably tolerable level of 50–70%. All that can be stated at present with complete confidence is that the total investment costs necessary for proper wastewater treatment, disposal and management are likely to be astronomical, and most developing countries would find it extremely difficult to meet these very high resource requirements in a timely manner.

Lack of Investment in Water Rehabilitation Projects

The second possible crisis is likely to come from lack of investments for both water quantity and quality considerations. Investment requirements for wastewater treatment have already been mentioned. These are for point sources only; investment needs for controlling non-point sources of pollution such as agricultural run-off are simply unknown at present, even for the Organization for Economic Co-operation and Development countries, let alone for developing countries. In addition, most existing water development projects in developing countries need massive investments for rehabilitation and modernization, and then for their efficient and sustainable operation. Equally, new projects are becoming increasingly expensive to develop because more efficient project sites have already been developed, or are in the process of development, and because of the social and environmental countermeasures necessary to reduce, or even eliminate, the anticipated adverse impacts. Analyses of current cost estimates for the next generation of water supply projects in developing countries indicate that these are likely to be 1.75–3 times the cost of the present generation of projects, in real terms and per cubic metre of water delivered. These high costs are still not adequately reflected in the current budget estimates of nearly all water agencies of the developing world, which is further distorting the levels of investments that will be required.

Globally, the total investment costs for modernizing and efficiently managing existing water development projects and wastewater treatment plants and to construct new ones are likely to be astronomical. Currently, not even 'ballpark' estimates of such costs are available. Thus, an important question is from what source would such financial investments be available? Governments all over the world now have high national debts and the resource-generating capacities of most developing countries and countries in transition, where most of the water projects have to be rehabilitated and the new ones are to be constructed, are limited. Moreover, the World Bank and the regional development banks have steadily reduced their financial support to water development projects as a percentage of their total loan portfolios in recent years. Furthermore, because of strong pressures from social and environmental activists, international financial institutions have become increasingly reluctant to finance new water development projects, irrespective of their overall societal benefits. In fact, a historian in the 21st century might very well conclude in a retrospective analysis that the Sardar Sarovar Project (Narmada Dam) in India became the World Bank's 'Viet Nam' in terms of its support to water projects during the 1990s. The regional development banks, which for all practical purposes follow the World Bank's leadership in most areas, have taken, at least unofficially, a very similar stance. There seems to be some rethinking going on in these institutions in terms of changing these politically expedient policies, but what is likely to be the actual policy during the next 10–20 years is anybody's guess. Thus, it is likely that unless the current situation improves very significantly, the lack of investments available may precipitate a water crisis as the 21st century progresses, from both water quantity and quality considerations.

Periodical Bibliography

The following articles have been selected to supplement the diverse views presented in this chapter.

Ronald Bailey   "Peak Oil Panic," *Reason*, May 2006.

Economist   "Empty Bowls, Heads, and Pockets," July 31, 2004.

Geographical   "Water Crisis Hitting World's Richest Nations," November 2006.

Chris Jozefowicz   "Water Boys," *Current Science*, January 19, 2007.

Shaena Montanari   "Global Climate Change Linked to Increasing World Hunger," *World Watch*, September/October 2005.

Mark Morrison, Stanley Reed, and Chris Palmeri   "Plenty of Oil—Just Drill Deeper," *Business Week*, September 18, 2006.

New Scientist   "Africa's Water Crisis Deepens," March 11, 2006.

Professional Engineering   "Oil Reserves Will Last for 41 Years, Says BP," June 23, 2004.

Jeffrey D. Sachs   "The Challenge of Sustainable Water," *Scientific American*, December 2006.

Stephen L. Sass   "Scarcity, Mother of Invention," *New York Times*, August 10, 2006.

Anita Inder Singh   "Governing Water Wisely," *UN Chronicle*, December/February 2006–2007.

David Strahan   "Who's Afraid of Peak Oil?" *Ecologist*, April 2007.

Alexandra Witze   "Energy: That's Oil, Folks . . ." *Nature*, January 4, 2007.

CHAPTER 2

What Global Agricultural Policies Should Be Pursued?

Chapter Preface

According to critics of the industrial farming methods used to grow and harvest huge sectors of the worldwide food supply, the processes involved are environmentally unfriendly and cannot be sustained indefinitely. The complaints about industrial methods include the erosion of topsoil, the rapid depletion of topsoil nutrients, and the heavy use of pesticides that critics insist may lead to human health problems. In addition, detractors charge that the intensive use of machinery and the irrigation runoff of pesticides and inorganic fertilizers add to pollution problems that have environmental impacts beyond the boundaries of these farms.

To offset or perhaps end the perceived problems of industrial agriculture, many farmers and environmentalists are advocating sustainable agricultural practices. Unlike its industrial counterpart, sustainable agriculture focuses on protecting soils, limiting tillage, recycling water, employing organic fertilizers, and keeping pesticide use to a minimum. Such ecological stewardship does not typically yield the size of crops that industrial farms are capable of producing, but advocates of sustainable agriculture have a different vision of the role of farms in the global food supply. As the National Sustainable Agriculture Information Service states, "In contrast to monocropped industrial megafarms that ship throughout the world, the vision of sustainable agriculture's futurists is small to mid-size diversified farms supplying the majority of their region's food." Using this paradigm, promoters of sustainable methods suggest that global food needs primarily can be met locally instead of relying on large combines to send less-than-fresh food over long distances. Some shipping would still need to be done, however, for food products that are not indigenous to a specific area and to meet the needs of people who live in countries that have poor agricultural environments.

Some critics oppose the transition to sustainable agriculture. They argue that the crop yields are significantly lower than those generated by industrial farming methods, meaning that less food would be produced overall unless more land was converted into farmland. This line of thinking angers commentators such as Dennis T. Avery, a director at the Hudson Institute, a think tank located in Indianapolis. In his book *Saving the Planet with Pesticides and Plastic*, Avery contends that "high-yield farming feeds the world on 5.8 million acres of land . . . whereas low-yield organic farming would require 15–16 million acres." Much of this now uncultivated land, Avery asserts, would have to be carved out of developing nations where starving populations are in need of food but also where protected wildlife refuges and environmentally sensitive regions are most plentiful. For such reasons, Avery and others insist that high-yield industrial farming is the better option for making sure that as much food is produced as possible to meet global needs.

In chapter 2, critics and commentators debate the value of sustainable agricultural practices in a world that still faces widespread hunger. They likewise address whether genetically modified food is safe enough to help feed starving millions or whether it will only add to global problems through unforeseen consequences of its use.

| "*Organic agriculture is the quickest, most efficient, most cost-effective and fairest way to feed the world.*"

Organic Agriculture Can Feed the World

Andre Leu

Andre Leu is the president of the Organic Producers Association of Queensland, Australia, and the chair of the Organic Federation of Australia. He argues in favor of organic agricultural practices in this viewpoint. According to Leu, organic farming is better than conventional farming because it does not rely on expensive fertilizers and pesticides and has no ill effects on the environment. Organic methods have yielded large harvests that can compete with the output of conventional factory farms, he writes, and organic agriculture can also be practiced anywhere in the world, because it is affordable. If nations utilized more arable land for organic agriculture, Leu claims, global hunger might be prevented.

As you read, consider the following questions:

1. According to Leu, what are North America, Australia, and Brazil doing to much of their prime arable farmland instead of using it to grow food?

Andre Leu, "Organic Agriculture Can Feed the World," *AcresUSA*, vol. 34, no. 1, January 2004. Reproduced by permission.

2. How has the introduction of more labor-intensive farming practices (associated with organic methods) benefited local economies, in Leu's opinion?

3. According to the cited investigation by Jules Pretty (in his book *The Living Land*), by what percentage can American organic farmers cut their use of pesticides and fertilizers?

Several high-profile advocates of conventional agricultural production have stated that the world would starve if we all converted to organic agriculture. They have written articles for science journals and other publications saying that organic agriculture is not sustainable and produces yields that are significantly lower than conventional agriculture.

Thus, the push for genetically modified organisms [GMOs], growth hormones, animal-feed antibiotics, food irradiation and toxic synthetic chemicals is being justified, in part, by the rationale that without these products the world will not be able to feed itself.

Warnings of Coming Global Starvation

Ever since Thomas Malthus wrote *An Essay on the Principle of Population* in 1798 and first raised the specter of overpopulation, various experts have been predicting the end of human civilization because of mass starvation.

The theme was popularized again by Paul Ehrlich in his 1968 book, *The Population Bomb*. According to Ehrlich's logic, we should all be starving now that the 21st century has arrived: "The battle to feed all of humanity is over. In the 1970s the world will undergo famines; hundreds of millions of people are going to starve to death in spite of any crash programs embarked upon now"

The only famines that have occurred since 1968 have been in African countries saddled with corrupt governments, political turmoil, civil wars and periodic droughts. The world had enough food for these people—it was political and logistical events that prevented them from producing adequate food or stopped aid from reaching them. Hundreds of millions of people did not starve to death.

The specter of mass starvation is being pushed again as the motive for justifying GMOs. In June 2003, President Bush stated at a biotechnology conference, "We should encourage the spread of safe, effective biotechnology to win the fight against global hunger."

We must now ask ourselves: Is global hunger due to a shortage of food production?

Shifting Agricultural Economies

In this first decade of the 21st century, many farmers around the world are facing a great economic crisis of low commodity prices. These low prices are due to oversupply. Current economic theories hold that prices decrease when supply is greater than demand.

Most of our current production systems are price driven, with the need for economies of scale to reduce unit costs. The small profit margins of this economic environment favor enterprises working in terms of large volume, and as a result the family farm is declining. Many areas of the United States and Australia have fewer farmers now than 100 years ago, and the small rural centers they support are disappearing. Hundreds of thousands of farmers have had to leave their farms in Argentina due to higher production costs and lower commodity prices. The sugar industry in Australia is on the verge of collapse for the same reason. Australian dairy farmers continue to leave the industry since deregulation forced down the prices they receive. Most of the major industrial countries are subsidizing their farmers so that their agricultural sectors do not collapse.

Losing Good Farmland

Europe, North America, Australia and Brazil are in the process of converting a large percentage of their arable land from food production to biofuels such as ethanol in an effort to establish viable markets for their farmers. The latest push in GMO development is BioPharm, in which plants such as corn, sugarcane and tobacco are modified to produce new compounds such as hormones, vaccines, plastics, polymers and other non-food compounds. All of these developments will mean that less food is grown on some of the world's most productive farmland.

Grain farmers in India have protested about cheap imports that are sending them deeper into poverty. Countries such as India and China, once considered as over-populated basket cases, export large quantities of food. In fact, India, one of the world's most populated countries, is a net food exporter in most years.

South American rainforests are cleared for pasture that is grazed with beef destined for the hamburger chains of North America. Once the soil is depleted, new areas are cleared for pasture and old, degraded areas are abandoned to weeds. In Asia, most of the forests are cleared for timber that is exported to the developed industrial economies. One of the saddest things about this massive, wasteful destruction of biodiversity is that very little of the newly cleared land is used to feed the poor. Most of this production of timber and beef is exported to the world's richest economies.

The reality is that the world produces more than enough food to feed everyone and has more than enough suitable agricultural land to do it. Unfortunately, due to inefficient, unfair distribution systems and poor farming methods, millions of people do not receive adequate nutrition.

Organic Methods at Work

Organic agriculture needs to be able to answer two major questions:

1. Can organic agriculture produce high yields?
2. Can organic agriculture get the food to the people who need it?

An editorial in *New Scientist* for February 3, 2001, stated that low-tech, sustainable agriculture is increasing crop yields on poor farms across the world, often by 70 percent or more. This has been achieved by replacing synthetic chemicals with natural pest control and natural fertilizers.

Professor Jules Pretty, director of the Centre for Environment and Society at the University of Essex, wrote, "Recent evidence from 20 countries has found more than 2 million families farming sustainably on more than 4–5 million hectares. This is no longer marginal. It cannot be ignored. What is remarkable is not so much the numbers, but that most of this has happened in the past 5–10 years. Moreover, many of the improvements are occurring in remote and resource-poor areas that had been assumed to be incapable of producing food surpluses." . . .

- 223,000 farmers in southern Brazil using green manures and cover crops of legumes and livestock integration have doubled yields of maize and wheat to 4–5 tons/hectare.

- 45,000 farmers in Guatemala and Honduras used regenerative technologies to triple maize yields to 2–2.5 tons/ha and diversify their upland farms, which has led to local economic growth that has in turn encouraged remigration back from the cities.

- 200,000 farmers across Kenya as part of sustainable agriculture programs have more than doubled their maize yields to about 2.5 to 3.3 tons/ha and substantially improved vegetable production through the dry seasons.

- 100,000 small coffee farmers in Mexico have adopted fully organic production methods and increased yields by half.

- A million wetland rice farmers in Bangladesh, China, India, Indonesia, Malaysia, Philippines, Sri Lanka, Thailand and Vietnam have shifted to sustainable agriculture, where group-based farmer field schools have enabled farmers to learn alternatives to pesticides and increase their yields by about 10 percent. . . .

Improving Local Livelihoods

One of the most important aspects of teaching farmers in these regions to increase yields with sustainable/organic methods is that the food and fiber is produced close to where it is needed and in many cases by the people who need it. It is not produced halfway around the world, transported and then sold to them.

Another important aspect is the low input costs. Growers do not need to buy expensive imported fertilizers, herbicides and pesticides. The increase in yields also comes with lower production costs, allowing a greater profit to these farmers.

Third, the substitution of more labor-intensive activities such as cultural weeding, composting and intercropping for expensive imported chemical inputs provides more employment for local and regional communities. This employment allows landless laborers to pay for their food and other needs. . . .

Benefits to Developed Nations

Since 1946, the advent of chemical fertilizers, pesticides, herbicides, improved crop varieties and industrial paradigms are

Sustainable Agriculture in Urban Areas

The emergence of food-producing community gardens in New York City reflects a trend that's taking root around the world. It's called urban agriculture. According to the Urban Agriculture Network, a non-governmental organization that supports urban agriculture development worldwide, more than a third of the world's urban areas are used for farming, with U.S. metropolitan areas producing more than 30 percent of the dollar value of domestic agricultural production. Urban food production is particularly strong in developing countries, where people rely on it to survive. But it's catching on in developed countries, too.

The rise of urban agriculture, experts say, may be in response to the expansion of cities and the loss of cropland. With diminishing arable land acreage, the theory goes, the conversion of unused lots of urban land into food production areas becomes increasingly important. Interestingly, urban agriculture marks a return to early cities, where food production was part and parcel of daily life.

Margarida Correia, "Harvest in the City,"
Earth Island Journal, *vol. 20, no. 3, Autumn 2005.*
http://earthisland.org/eijournal/
new_articles.cfm?articleID=979&journalID;=84.

credited with producing the high yields of the "green revolution." Because organic agriculture avoids many of these new inputs, it is assumed that it always results in lower yields.

The assumption that greater inputs of synthetic chemical fertilizers and pesticides are required to increase food yields is not accurate. In a study published in *The Living Land*, Professor Pretty looked at projects in seven industrialized countries of Europe and North America. He reported, "Farmers are finding that they can cut their inputs of costly pesticides and fertilizers substantially, varying from 20 to 80 percent, and be financially better off. Yields do fall to begin with (by 10 to 15 percent, typically), but there is compelling evidence that they soon rise and go on increasing. In the U.S.A., for example, the top quarter of sustainable agriculture farmers now have higher yields than conventional farmers, as well as a much lower negative impact on the environment."

Professor George Monbiot, in an article in the *Guardian* (August 24, 2000), wrote that wheat grown with manure has produced consistently higher yields for the past 150 years than wheat grown with chemical nutrients, in U.K. trials.

A study of apple production conducted by Washington State University compared the economic and environmental sustainability of conventional, organic and integrated growing systems in apple production. The organic system had equivalent yields to the other systems. The study also showed that the break-even point was nine years after planting for the organic system and 15 and 16 years, respectively, for conventional and integrated farming systems.

In an article published in the peer-reviewed scientific journal *Nature*, Laurie Drinkwater and colleagues from the Rodale Institute showed that organic farming had better environmental outcomes as well as similar yields of both products and profits when compared to conventional, intensive agriculture. . . .

The Best Solution

Organic agriculture is viable [as a method of] preventing global hunger because:

- It can achieve high yields.

- It can achieve these yields in the areas where it is needed most.

- It has low inputs.

- It is cost-effective and affordable.

- It provides more employment so that the impoverished can purchase [what they] need.

- It does not require any expensive technical investment.

It costs tens of millions of dollars and takes many years to develop *one* genetically modified plant variety. This money would be spent far more productively on organic agricultural education, research and extension in the areas where we need to overcome hunger and poverty.

Organic agriculture is the quickest, most efficient, most cost-effective and fairest way to feed the world.

> "[O]rganic farming is mining the soil of its vital minerals, particularly phosphorus and potassium. . . . Conventional farming, on the other hand, restores mineral balances through fertilization."

Organic Agriculture Cannot Feed the World

Ronald Bailey

Ronald Bailey is a science correspondent for Reason, *a leading libertarian monthly magazine. In this viewpoint, Bailey argues that organic agriculture cannot produce enough crops to satisfy global demand. Quoting a 2002 Swiss study, Bailey states that organic farming has lower crop yields than conventional agriculture and that the food generated contains fewer nutrients. He maintains that the widespread use of artificially produced fertilizers is responsible for the abundance of farm crops, while, conversely, organic fertilization methods can only produce food on a small scale. If the world's agricultural industry converted to organic practices, Bailey contends, global populations would suffer.*

Ronald Bailey, "Organic Alchemy: Organic Farming Could Kill Billions of People," *Reason*, June 5, 2002. Reproduced by permission.

As you read, consider the following questions:

1. In addition to synthetic fertilizers, what other inventions does Bailey cite as important to boosting food supplies?

2. According to Bailey, what is the difference between "natural" sources of nitrogen, phosphorous, and potassium and "artificial" sources of these elements?

3. What is no-till farming, and what are some of its benefits according to the author?

Organic food production is growing by leaps and bounds in the United States. Many consumers are willing to pay premium prices for organic fruits, vegetables, and meats, convinced that they are helping the earth and eating healthier.

[In 2002] Swiss scientists at the Research Institute for Organic Agriculture ... published a 21-year study in *Science* comparing two types of organic farming with two types of conventional agriculture. The results initially seem to back up those consumer beliefs, and the press has described the research as showing that organic farms are "viable" (to quote the *Los Angeles Times*) and "more efficient" (to quote Reuters). But don't rush out just yet to Whole Foods to stock up on organic arugula or chard.

Organic Is Not Superior

Organic farming boils down to essentially two principles: Soluble mineral inputs, such as artificial nitrogen fertilizer, are forbidden, and so is the use of synthetic herbicides and pesticides. Another of the organic systems tested by the Swiss scientists, called bio-dynamic, was dreamed up by the German "anthroposophist" mystic Rudolf Steiner in the 1920s. Biodynamic farming uses such novel preparations as manure fermented in a cow's horn that is buried in the soil for six months through autumn and winter. [Adding to] these original principles, organic farmers' organizations have recently proscribed growing genetically enhanced crops.

The Problems of Land and Manure Use

Organic farming takes up much more land than conventional farming. It is naive to think that organic farming can feed the "world." Organic farming requires manure, which requires animals, which requires forage land. Today [2000] there are 6.5 billion people on the face of the earth. By 2050, we may have 10 billion people. Because organic farming uses nitrogen in manure, they will have to produce significantly more manure to keep up with the demand to feed 3–4 billion more people. It cannot be done. In fact, all of the world's cultivatable land has already been taken up. In order to increase food production the key is to increase yield—grow more plants on the same or smaller space. Organic farming can use higher yielding varieties (developed by conventional breeding). However the demand for manure is too great. It has been estimated, that, at most, organic farming practices can feed 4 billion people. We have passed that already.

Bob Goldberg,
"The Hypocrisy of Organic Farmers," AgBio World, June 5, 2000.
www.agbioworld.org/biotech-info/articles/biotech-art/hypocrisy.html.

One of the most frequent criticisms of organic agriculture is that it is not as productive as conventional farming. The Swiss scientists confirmed this: Their organic plots were on average 20 percent less productive than conventional plots. For potatoes, organic production was about 40 percent lower. The researchers also point out that "cereal crop yields in Europe typically are 60 to 70% of those under conventional management." Furthermore, they dispelled the notion that organic crops are superior food by noting, "There were minor differences between the farming systems in food quality."

The Swiss scientists based their claims for greater organic "efficiency" chiefly on the differences in the amount of energy used to produce the crops. Since the same horticultural techniques were used on both conventional and organic plots, the difference in energy use was mostly the result of counting the energy used to produce inorganic fertilizers and pesticides. On this basis, the researchers claim in their *Science* article that organic farms use about 50 percent less energy. However, looking at the fine print, one discovers that "since crop yields were considerably higher in the conventional systems, the difference in energy needed to produce a crop unit was only 19 percent lower in the organic systems."

Secondly, the researchers declare that they found nutrients "in the organic systems to be 34 to 51% lower than in conventional systems, whereas mean crop yield was only 20% lower over a period of 21 years." But—to ask the organic advocates' own question—is organic agriculture sustainable over the long run? Again, the fine print says no. As their research confirms, organic farming is mining the soil of its vital minerals, particularly phosphorus and potassium. Eventually, as these minerals are used up, organic crop production will fall below its already low level. Conventional farming, on the other hand, restores mineral balances through fertilization.

Synthetic Fertilizer Is Needed to Raise Crops for Global Consumption

"The Swiss researchers are not thinking globally, they're only acting locally," says Alex Avery, director of research for the Hudson Institute's Center for Global Food Issues. Avery points out that organic farming can supply food for niche markets of affluent consumers but cannot feed a hungry world. Other methods of food production can. In his new book *Enriching the Earth*, the University of Manitoba agronomist Vaclav Smil credits the Haber-Bosch method of producing nitrogen fertilizer, invented in 1909, with sustaining two billion people today.

Synthetic fertilizers now supply 40 percent of all the nitrogen used by crop plants. Without this artificially produced fertilizer, farmers would simply not be able to grow the crops necessary to feed the world's population. Organic sources of nitrogen, such as animal manure and leguminous plants, would supply only about a quarter of the nitrogen needed. (The remainder comes from rain and lightning.) Other inventions, such as high-yielding crop varieties and modern farm equipment, have also been vital to boosting food supplies. For example, when farm tractors arrived after the 1920s, they replaced draft animals that consumed a quarter of the crops grown in the United States.

Keep in mind that plants cannot tell the difference between "natural" sources of nitrogen, phosphorus, and potassium and "artificial" sources of those elements. The reason is that there *is* no difference, outside the minds of organic farmers.

Benefits of No-Till Farming

The Swiss researchers did find some true benefits from organic farming, including greater water retention by the soil and a higher presence of beneficial insects. Unfortunately, they did not test their organic systems against the newest form of conventional agriculture, no-till farming combined with genetically enhanced crops. This uses much less energy and less pesticides than the old-fashioned systems examined by the Swiss scientists.

Since no-till farmers don't plow, their tractors use less fuel. Also, since weed control is achieved using environmentally benign herbicides instead of mechanical removal through plowing, even more fuel is saved. Finally, no-till farmers use less insecticide, since genetically enhanced crops can protect themselves against pests. Against all this, organic farming's 19 percent energy advantage would likely disappear.

No-till farming matches several other advantages of organic agriculture as well. Both methods offer improved soil structure, more water retention, greatly reduced soil erosion, less pesticide and fertilizer runoff, and a higher presence of beneficial insects. Although organic farmers refuse to see it, switching to genetically enhanced crops would go a long way toward accomplishing their avowed goals of restoring their land and helping the natural environment.

Negative Consequences

One final argument often offered by organic enthusiasts is that organic farming is more profitable. Of course, the reason organic foods command a premium at supermarkets is that so many consumers have been bamboozled into thinking that they are somehow superior. If organic farming became widespread, that premium would dissipate and take its higher profitability with it.

As the Cambridge chemist John Emsley recently concluded, "The greatest catastrophe that the human race could face this century is not global warming but a global conversion to 'organic farming'—an estimated 2 billion people would perish." News reports may hail the Swiss study as proving that organic farming is sustainable, but it actually did the opposite.

> "Starvation is much more dangerous to more people than any threat presented by GM foods."

Genetically Modified Foods Should Be Produced to Feed the World

African American Environmentalist Association

In this viewpoint, the African American Environmentalist Association (AAEA) insists that genetically modified (GM) foods are a beneficial innovation that are helping feed hungry populations across the globe. The AAEA believes that GM foods are proven safe and have the advantage of being engineered hardier and more resilient than natural varieties. As long as regulatory bodies exist to oversee the production of GM foods, the AAEA argues that they should continue to be dispersed throughout the marketplace. The African American Environmentalist Association, founded in 1985, is a national, nonprofit environmental organization. The Association encourages African American participation in the environmental movement.

African American Environmentalist Association, "Genetically Modified Foods," 2005. Reproduced by permission.

As you read, consider the following questions:

1. According to the AAEA, why are some social justice groups opposing shipments of GM food aid to African countries?

2. What are some of the benefits of GM foods, as the AAEA states?

3. According to the AAEA, how has the U.S. Food and Drug Administration assessed GM foods in comparison to non-GM foods?

The terms genetically modified (GM) or genetically engineered (GE) foods and genetically modified organisms (GMOs) refer to crop plants created for human or animal consumption using the latest molecular biology techniques. These techniques of modern genetics have made possible the direct manipulation of the genetic makeup of organisms. Combining genes from different organisms is known as recombinant DNA technology and the resulting organism is said to be "genetically modified," "genetically engineered," or "transgenic." ... Like most human planetary management issues today, such as global climate change, the GM foods issue is hugely complex. GM foods have great promise and great dangers. AAEA leans in the direction of aggressive market production with needed oversight regulations in a global management context. If all goes well, one thing is certain, we will have to feed about 12 billion people every day in the next 50 years.

Making a Moral Choice

Good and evil are moral choices humans are free to make. As applied to technology, these moral choices present great opportunities and great dangers. We manipulate atoms to light our buildings and to make weapons of mass destruction. Companies produce chemicals to make our lives easier, but sometimes cut corners in the management, storage and disposal to maximize profits. We utilize coal, oil and gas for our cars, businesses and utility needs, but these same natural resources pollute our air and water without adequate protections. Twenty-first century choices face us in stem cell research, cloning and genetically modified foods. Proponents and opponents present their cues and policy makers are faced with protecting the public interest. Unfortunately, human history is littered with cases of indiscretions by people with evil intentions. It is within this context that we look at the case for genetically modified and engineered organisms and foods.

We support prudent use of genetically modified foods. We believe that labels should be placed on all GM products. We also understand the risks involved, but believe the benefits far outweigh the costs. Starvation is much more dangerous to more people than any threat presented by GM foods. Droughts and famine are increasing throughout the world, particularly on the continent of Africa. Although some traditional environmental groups insist that they are simply providing facts about potential health and environmental effects of GM foods, others oppose it as a Frankenstein product. Of course, none of these groups have programs to feed the world's hungry. Some USA-based social justice groups, such as the Africa Faith & Justice Network are opposing USA policies that impose GM food aid on southern African countries facing severe drought and famine. In addition to concerns about health effects, they think it is a tactic to blatantly benefit agri-business, not poor and hungry people. We understand the health concerns, but see nothing wrong with agri-business profiting from such exchanges. Capitalism feeds America. In fact, Americans are suffering more from overeating than lack of food. As planetary managers, we must understand that there are no benign systems that can provide for human needs and we are obligated to protect the planet to the maximum extent possible. One major advantage of GM food is that crops genetically engineered to resist weeds and bugs enable farmers to decrease pesticide and herbicide use. Of course, superweeds and bugs could also be inadvertently created. Planetary management is very complex and serious business.

The European Corn Debate

The fight over the use of genetically modified corn provides a good example to illustrate the issues involved in the use of this product. Interestingly, one of the leading opponents to new GM produce, Europe, has preliminarily approved (January 2004) the sale of GM corn via the European Commission. . . . Opponents promise to sue to stop the use of GM corn in the EU [European Union]. Environmental opponents believe GM products threaten biodiversity and will release potentially harmful contaminants into the environment. We support Friend of the Earth's proposed "GM Contamination and Liability Bill" being introduced in the British Parliament. The bill calls for a strict approach to any future planting of GM crops, including those planted for trial purposes. It stipulates minimum separation distances between GM and organic/conventional crops, clarifies liability issues if cross-contamination occurs, and ensures the regulation of GM is simple and that all overseeing bodies are self-funded. We do not support the Five-Year Freeze associated with the bill.

Unrealized Fears of GM Crops

Genetically modified [food] will not eliminate hunger and malnutrition, because dysfunctional governments and economies create problems with production, access and distribution of food. Flawed policies, greed and incompetence will always keep some people in ignorance and poverty. However, GM foods can improve survivability and increase productivity of plants in inhospitable conditions. GM foods can also reduce the need to use large quantities of herbicides and pesticides. Of course, this does not stop Mendocino County, California—considered by some to be the center of America's anti-

Better and More Abundant Food

By manipulating plants . . . with [genetic engineering] technology, scientists will be able to produce more nutritious and healthy food, with higher protein and vitamin contents.

New varieties of fruit and vegetables will be created that will enrich our choices and delight our taste. We soon might even see food especially engineered to combat disease, by methods such as incorporating disease fighting elements or vaccines into it.

It is worthy of note that increased yields will follow as a direct consequence of fewer losses in better protected crops, making food cheaper and more plentiful in the future.

David Holcberg,
"Is Genetically Engineered Food Good or Bad for You?"
Capitalism Magazine, *March 5, 2001. www.capmag.com.*

biotechnology movement—from holding a vote to prohibit GM plants and animals from being raised or kept in the county. Such anti-GM entities consider it to be the biggest uncontrolled biological experiment going on in the world today. Although proof of serious harm to humans, animals and plants has yet to be definitively proven, opponents fear that humans and the environment could be damaged through accidental cross-pollination of GM products with natural plants. This is a legitimate fear, but is not sufficient to ban the use of all GM products. Proponents point out that negative effects are nonexistent, pointing out that not a single stomach ache has been reported since the Food and Drug Administration first approved genetically engineered crops for human consumption in 1994. Great Britain's Food Standards Agency also favors the use of GM foods. Of course, most health effects of concern, including cancer and the results of long-term damage to the immune system, take years to become evident. And then there would be the complex task of directly associating any damaging effects with GM products.

Hardy, Safe GM Foods

All types of foods and organisms have been genetically engineered: corn, cotton, tomatoes, soybeans, sugarbeets, oilseed rape, maize, salmon, pigs, cows, and the list goes on. With about 6 billion people eating every day, we need every reasonable tool known to man to assure adequate nutrition for Earth's residents. GM foods, property utilized, can help meet these needs in a number of ways: pest resistance, herbicide tolerance, disease resistance, cold tolerance, drought tolerance and salinity tolerance, among others. Many countries are growing GM crops: U.S., Canada, China, Argentina, Australia, Bulgaria, France, Germany, Mexico, Romania, South Africa, Spain and Uruguay. Interestingly, according the USDA [United States Department of Agriculture] approximately 54% of all soybeans cultivated in the U.S. in 2000 were genetically modified. In the U.S., three government agencies have jurisdiction over GM foods: EPA [Environmental Protection Agency] evaluates GM plants for environmental safety, the USDA evaluates whether the plant is safe to grow, and the FDA [Food and Drug Administration] evaluates whether the plant is safe to eat.

Mandatory food labeling is also a complex issue. The FDA's,current position on food labeling is govered by the Food, Drug and Cosmetic Act, which is only concerned with food additives, not whole foods or food products that are considered GRAS (Generally Recognized As Safe). The FDA contends that GM foods are substantially equivalent to non-GM foods, and therefore not subject to more stringent labeling. If all GM foods and food products are to be labeled, Congress must enact sweeping changes in the existing food labeling policy. The Genetically Engineered Food Right to Know Act (HR 2916) is probably a good place to start for food labeling.

Oversight Is Still Needed

Just as AAEA supports nuclear power with the belief that there should be serious oversight, we support the use of modified foods in the same way. We believe that traditional environmental groups go [too] far in calling for a ban on nuclear power and GM. They could still provide 95% of the same constructive criticisms and oversight in these areas, but are extremist when calling for bans on useful, relatively safe products. We understand that part of this extremism partially comes as a reaction to the extremism of greedy, unscrupulous capitalists abusers. As part of a minority group with a long history of disadvantage, we do not have time for these games. However, we have serious concerns about human genetic engineering, particularly cross-species modifications and cloning. We fear that the Hitlerian contingent will take experiments with human DNA into an area of manufacturing humans for some ungodly reason and mad scientists will inexorably attempt to pierce the species' genetic barrier and mix humans with animals FOR IMPROVEMENTS. Cinema has caught these images in *The Matrix* and *The Island of Dr. Moreau*. We would join our extremist colleagues in the traditional environmental movement in calling for a total ban on this type of unethical and immoral activity.

| "GM foods may create unpredicted and
potentially dangerous side effects."

Genetically Modified Foods Are Dangerous and Unneeded

Jeffrey Smith

Jeffrey Smith is the founding director of the Institute for Responsible Technology and has campaigned against the production of genetically modified (GM) foods for years. Smith details in the follow viewpoint why he believes GM foods are abnormal and potentially dangerous. According to Smith, since GM foods have not been part of agriculture for a substantial number of years, no long-term studies of their possible ill effects are available. Several short-term trials in animals and humans have shown deleterious effects of some GM foods. However, Smith contends that in America these results are routinely silenced by the GM industry, which also has influence in the policy making of the Food and Drug Administration and other government oversight organizations. Smith concludes by stating that because GM foods may be unhealthful, they should not be touted as a way to meet global food needs.

As you read, consider the following questions:

1. What happened to rats fed the GM FlavrSavr tomato, as Smith relates in his viewpoint?

2. As Smith explains, a deadly epidemic in the 1980s was supposedly traced to a food additive called L-tryptophan. How does Smith say the biotech industry diverted blame away from the GM enhancement in this case?

3. In Smith's view, who ultimately determines whether biotech foods are safe?

You probably eat genetically modified (GM) foods at every meal without knowing it. Most Americans do. While the biotech industry claims that the FDA [Food and Drug Administration] has thoroughly evaluated GM foods and found them safe, internal FDA documents made public from a lawsuit reveal that agency scientists warned that GM foods might create toxins, allergies, nutritional problems, and new diseases that might be difficult to identify.

GM Foods Are Not Proven Safe

Genetically modified foods are those which have foreign genes inserted into their DNA. While scientists originally assumed that the inserted genes would only add a particular desired trait to the crop, new evidence suggests that the host's normal natural genes can get switched off, turned on permanently, damaged, or altered in the process. And that's just some of the many ways that GM foods may create unpredicted and potentially dangerous side effects.

A January 2001 report from an expert panel of the Royal Society of Canada said it was "scientifically unjustifiable" to presume that GM foods are safe, and that the "default prediction" for any GM foods is the creation of unintended side effects. They called for safety testing, looking for short- and long-term human toxicity, allergenicity, and other health effects.

Unfortunately, there have been very few safety studies. Of the 10 published animal feeding studies, the most in-depth one showed evidence of damaged immune systems, digestive problems, excessive cell growth, and stunted organ development in rats fed an experimental GM potato. The scientist identified the process of genetic modification as the probable cause—the same process used in creating most GM food on the market. When the scientist went public with his findings, he was fired from his job after 35 years, and silenced with threats of a lawsuit. Unfortunately, no published study has yet tested the GM foods on the market to see if they create these same damaging effects in laboratory animals or humans.

Dangerous Consequences

Rats fed the genetically modified FlavrSavr tomato developed stomach lesions. Seven of forty rats died within two weeks. The crop was approved, but has since been taken off the market.

The only human feeding trial ever conducted confirmed that genetically engineered genes from soy burgers and a soy milkshake transferred to the bacteria inside the digestive tract after only one meal, making the bacteria resistant to herbicide. (The biotech industry had previously said that such a transfer was impossible.) The World Health Organization, the British and American Medical Associations, and several other groups have expressed concern that if the "antibiotic resistant marker genes" used in GM foods got transferred to bacteria, it could create *super-diseases* that are immune to antibiotics.

In the 1980's a deadly epidemic was traced to the food supplement L-tryptophan, created from genetically modified bacteria. About 100 Americans died and an estimated 5–10,000 fell sick—some were permanently disabled. Biotech proponents successfully diverted the blame away from genetic engineering by attributing the disease to changes in the filtration system at the factory. It is now known, however, that hundreds had contracted the disease from genetically modified versions of L-tryptophan created during the four years prior to the change in the filter.

The disease created by the contaminated L-tryptophan was acute, rare, and came on quickly. If all three of these characteristics had not been present, it is unlikely that doctors would have identified the supplement as the cause; it might still be on the market. This [situation provokes] the question, "Are there other genetically modified products on the market creating serous health problems that are not being traced?"

Increasing Risks of Disease

According to a March 2001 report, the U.S. Centers for Disease Control says that food is responsible for twice the number of illnesses in the U.S. compared to estimates just seven years earlier. This increase roughly corresponds to the period when Americans have been eating lots of newly introduced GM foods. Could that be contributing to the 5,000 deaths, 325,000 hospitalizations, and 76 million illnesses related to food each year? It's hard to say since there is no monitoring in place.

In the UK—one of the few places that do annual evaluations of allergy statistics—soy allergies skyrocketed by 50% immediately after GM soy was imported for the first time from the United States. This might have resulted from the increased allergen, trypsin inhibitor, in the genetically modified Roundup Ready® soy or perhaps from the protein in that soy that has never before been part of the human food supply.

Milk and dairy products from cows treated with the genetically engineered bovine growth hormone (bGH) contain an increased amount of the hormone IGF-1, which is one of the highest risk factors associated with breast and prostate

Forcing GM Food on Developing Nations

Even food aid is being used to push GM foods. It is no longer about humanitarian needs of starving populations but about the commercial interests of the international corporations. First finding an outlet for its mounting food surplus through the midday meal scheme for African children (force-fed through the World Food Programme), the U.S. then literally arm-twisted four African countries to accept GM food at the height of the food scarcity that prevailed in central and southern Africa in 2002. . . .

It did not, however, work. Zambia and Zimbabwe led the resistance against GM foods, saying that they would prefer their poor to die than to feed them with unhealthy food. Meanwhile, Sudan too has decided not to accept GM food aid.

The U.S. has therefore found a way to force the African countries into submission. The U.S. Senate has passed a bill, "the United States Leadership Against HIV/AIDS, Tuberculosis, and Malaria Act of 2003," which in a diplomatic way (calling it as 'sense of Congress') links financial aid for combating HIV/AIDS with GM food acceptance.

Devinder Sharma, "GM Foods: Towards an Apocalypse,"
ZNet, July 19, 2003. www.zmag.org.

cancer. The Council on Scientific Affairs of the American Medical Association called for more studies to determine if ingesting "higher than normal concentrations of [IGF-1] is safe for children, adolescents, and adults." In addition, Sam Epstein, M.D., chairman of the Cancer Prevention Coalition and author of eight books, wrote, "bGH and its digested products could be absorbed from milk into blood, particularly in infants, and produce hormonal and allergic effects." He described how "cell-stimulating growth factors . . . could induce premature growth and breast stimulation in infants, and possibly promote breast cancer in adults."

Silencing the Opposition

One of the most dangerous aspects of genetic engineering is the closed thinking and consistent effort to silence those with contrary evidence or concerns. Just before stepping down from office, former Secretary of Agriculture Dan Glickman admitted the following:

> "What I saw generically on the pro-biotech side was the attitude that the technology was good, and that it was almost immoral to say that it wasn't good, because it was going to solve the problems of the human race and feed the hungry and clothe the naked. . . . And there was a lot of money that had been invested in this, and if you're against it, you're Luddites, you're stupid. That, frankly, was the side our government was on. . . . You felt like you were almost an alien, disloyal, by trying to present an open-minded view."

Contrast this with the warning by the editors of *Nature Biotechnology*: "The risks in biotechnology are undeniable, and they stem from the unknowable in science and commerce. It is prudent to recognize and address those risks, not compound them by overly optimistic or foolhardy behavior."

In spite of such warnings and the mounting evidence of potential dangers, the FDA claims that GM foods are no different and do not require safety testing. A manufacturer can introduce a GM food without even informing the government or consumers. How could the agency put such a dangerous industry-friendly policy in place, when their own scientists had insisted that each GM variety should be subjected to long-term safety tests before being allowed on the market? One hint was that a former attorney to the biotech giant Monsanto was in charge of FDA policy making. Another hint comes from a memo by former FDA Commissioner David

Kessler, who described the agency's policy as "consistent with the general biotechnology policy established by the Office of the President." He said, "It also responds to White House interest in assuring the safe, speedy development of the U.S. biotechnology industry."

Gambling with Health

Thus, the biotech companies themselves determine if their own foods are safe. While they voluntarily submit studies, according to the Center for Science in the Public Interest, they contain "technical shortcomings in the safety data . . . as well as some obvious errors that the FDA failed to detect." There are also a handful of published industry-sponsored studies. But many scientists describe these as "designed to avoid finding any problems."

Many of the key assumptions used as the basis for industry and government safety claims have been proven wrong or remain untested. Although they continue to promote the myth that GM foods are needed to feed the world, according to the United Nations this is not true. Furthermore, GM crops increase reliance on agricultural chemicals and actually reduce average yields. I encourage you to ignore industry's vacuous claims and review the data for yourself. It provides a compelling case why these foods should never have been approved, and why eating them is gambling with your health.

"*Increasingly, a significant share of . . . fish is being grown by human-managed aquaculture fisheries. . . .*"

Fish Farming Can Help Feed the World

Food and Agriculture Organization of the United Nations

In this viewpoint, the Food and Agriculture Organization (FAO) of the United Nations maintains that aquaculture, which includes the farming of fish and other sea foods, is growing in proportion to the global demand for food. The FAO states that aquaculture is most prevalent in developing countries where food insecurity is a major social problem. This means that locally grown sea foods can reach nearby markets at affordable prices. In addition, the FAO notes that the fish farms in developing nations also help provide employment and trade for traditionally low-income populations. The FAO is the arm of the United Nations that dispenses agricultural information to nations in need and helps implement policies on national and international levels to contend with global hunger.

As you read, consider the following questions:

1. As FAO figures from 2000 state, what percent of essential animal proteins does the population of the Philippines get from fish?

2. In 2001, what percent of fish products sold internationally came from developing nations, according to the FAO?

3. According to FAO spokespeople, to what can most of the problems with global aquaculture be attributed?

More than one billion people worldwide rely on fish as a major source of animal proteins. Increasingly, a significant share of that fish is being grown by human-managed aquaculture fisheries—the majority of them located in those areas of the world most vulnerable to food insecurity.

Between 1970 and 2000, FAO figures show, aquaculture's contribution to global fisheries (in terms of shellfish and finfish production, not plants) increased nearly sevenfold, from 3.9 to 27 percent of the total. In 2000, the sector provided over 36 percent of the world's food-fish supplies.

The lion's share of global aquaculture production occurs in developing countries (90 percent of the total) and Low-Income Food Deficit Countries (LIFDCs, 81 percent). Indeed, annual growth of the sector in LIFDCs over the last three decades has been more than double that in developed countries.

And most of that production happens on small, family-managed fish farms.

"Just about 13 percent of production comes from what is sometimes called 'industrial aquaculture' and involves carnivorous species at the top of the food chain," notes Rohana Subasinghe, a Senior Fisheries Officer at FAO and secretary of the Committee on Fisheries's Sub-Committee on Aquaculture. "The bulk of production involves fish low on the food chain and occurs in developing countries, particularly in Asia, where aquaculture provides livelihoods and meets pressing food and nutrition needs."

Healthy and Affordable

For millions of people around the world, fish is a dietary mainstay. FAO figures for 2000 show that fish provided around 19 percent of total animal protein supplies in Africa, 21 percent in China and 23 percent in Asia. At the country level, the profile of fish in meeting nutritional needs can be even higher. In the Philippines, for example, the population gets 53 percent of essential animal proteins by eating fish.

"One of the main factors behind the high demand in developing countries for staple food fish—in particular inexpensive farmed freshwater fish species feeding low on the aquatic food chain—is their greater affordability to the poorer segments of the community," says Subasinghe.

But the benefits of eating fish add up to more than household economics. Even in small quantities, fish can tip the balance in terms of providing a healthy diet. It is a rich source of high-quality protein and a wide variety of vitamins and minerals, including vitamins A and D, phosphorus, magnesium, selenium and iodine. Similarly, the oils supplied by many fish species have a number of demonstrated dietary and health benefits.

Aquaculture and Poverty Alleviation

Beyond its direct role in the fight against hunger, aquaculture can also indirectly improve food security by reducing poverty, providing jobs and boosting foreign exchange earnings in the developing world.

Today, fish is one of the most traded international food products—the value of world fisheries production in 2001 was US$56 billion—and developing countries produce more than 50 percent of the fish and fishery products being sold internationally.

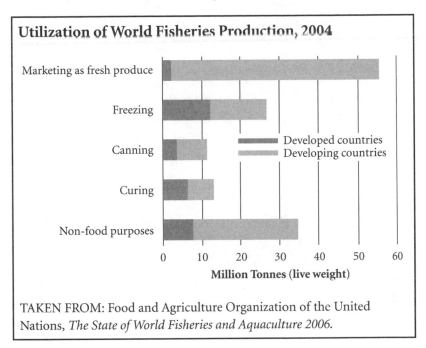

Utilization of World Fisheries Production, 2004

TAKEN FROM: Food and Agriculture Organization of the United Nations, *The State of World Fisheries and Aquaculture 2006.*

This means jobs. Aquaculture provides employment to millions of people worldwide, either directly or through affiliated industries that provide feed, equipment or services to fish farmers.

Total employment in the sector is highest in China, where it employs almost 4 million people full-time. In Viet Nam, where aquaculture employment is estimated at over 700,000 people, jobs in the catfish and shrimp sectors have in recent years provided an average annual household income of over US$1000—significantly more than that generated by comparable agriculture practices. The average annual household income nationwide in Viet Nam is about US$408.

Tackling Questions of Health and Safety

However, along with the benefits of aquaculture come challenges.

The globalization of the world food trade has put food safety front and centre in international debates. Fish products in general—and aquaculture products in particular—have been subject to close scrutiny for their safeness and environmental impacts.

Specific issues of concern include loss of natural habitats to shrimp farms, the spread of diseases and the use of antibiotics, the reliance on fishmeal from capture fisheries in some operations and the introduction of non-native species to local ecosystems.

"These are real problems. But we know that most of them stem from weak regulatory frameworks and too rapid development associated with the great commercial potential of some high-value species," says Serge Garcia, director of FAO's Fishery Resources Division. "Our focus needs to be on improving our understanding of the real impacts and causes, identifying the remedies and forging agreement on collective actions and responsible measures."

Sustainable and Responsible Aquaculture

"Challenges to sustainable development in aquaculture are only half the story," adds Subasinghe. "Important lessons have been learned. We have seen places where tremendous improvements in sustainable production have taken place."

To help tackle environmental and safety issues and chart out a course for the sustainable development of the aquaculture sector, FAO's Committee on Fisheries established an International Sub-Committee on Aquaculture in 2001. This body—over 50 different countries actively participate—meets regularly to take up issues of shared concern, shape the work of FAO's fisheries department and make recommendations regarding national and international policy related to aquaculture.

"The Sub-Committee has the responsibility to identify and debate key issues and develop practical, action-oriented recommendations," explains Garcia. "The ultimate objective is to ensure that this important sector is developed in a sustainable, responsible and equitable manner."

> *"If fish farming continues to grow at the current rate, then by 2010 the aquaculture industry could well be using all the world's fish oil and half its fishmeal."*

Fish Farming Is Environmentally Destructive

Emma Duncan

Emma Duncan is a former managing editor at the WWF International, the main secretariat of the network of global World Wildlife Fund for Nature (WWF) offices. In this viewpoint, Duncan contends that aquaculture is currently not a sustainable method of supplying food because of the demands it places on the environment. According to Duncan, fish farms consume more fish protein than they produce, draining already over-exploited feeder fish populations and much of the world's fish oil supplies. Duncan further claims that the loss of feeder fish threatens wild populations of larger fish and seabirds that prey on the small fish.

As you read, consider the following questions:

1. As Duncan states, what pelagic fish varieties are commonly used to make fishmeal for aquaculture?

Emma Duncan, "Fish Food for Thought," *World Wildlife Fund Newsroom*, February 18, 2003. Reproduced by permission.

2. According to Duncan's viewpoint, in what year were the North East Atlantic fisheries fully fished? In what year were they considered overfished?

3. What two alternatives does Duncan say might be adopted to replace the use of pelagic fish for fish-meal?

Each year, some 80 million tonnes of wild fish are caught from the world's oceans. But not all these fish end up on our dinner plates. More than one-third is used to make fish-meal and fish oil. Even this doesn't all go directly into food or other products: two-thirds goes to make feed for farmed fish.

Aquaculture is one of the fastest-growing food industries in the world. The growth of the fish farming sector of the industry is largely fuelled by an ever-increasing demand for high-quality fish such as salmon and trout. These are carnivorous fish that in the wild eat smaller fish, squid, and other crustaceans. When farmed, they are fed pellets made largely of fishmeal and fish oil.

Using Up Fish Products to Feed Aquaculture

Most fish oil and fishmeal is made from small, bony pelagic fish such as anchovies, pilchards, mackerel, herring, and whiting. Some species are also used for human consumption, but others, known as "industry fish", are only used for making these products.

The amount of feed needed for farmed fish is staggering. WWF has calculated that, as a conservative estimate, 4 kilograms of wild-caught fish are needed to produce 1 kilogram of farmed fish. The aquaculture industry currently consumes 70 per cent of the global production of fish oil and 34 per cent of total fishmeal. The salmon and trout fish farming sectors alone consume 53 per cent of the world's fish oil. And if fish farming continues to grow at the current rate, then by

Disease and Parasites Plague Fish Farmers

Disease is always a problem when fish are raised in close quarters. After a 1999 outbreak of infectious salmon anemia in fish farms in Scotland, all the farm-grown fish within 25 miles were slaughtered. A similar anemia outbreak in Maine [in 2000] led to the destruction of more than 2.5 million fish—and to federal insurance payouts totaling $16 million. "The more aquaculture there is," warns Callum Roberts, senior lecturer in marine conservation at the University of York in England, "the more disease there will be."

Parasite infestation is another chronic problem of high-density seafood farms. One of the most damaging organisms is the sea louse, which breeds by the millions in the vicinity of captive salmon. In 1989 Peter Mantle, who owns a wild salmon and sea-trout sport fishery in Delphi on the west coast of Ireland, discovered that young trout returning to his river from the ocean were covered with lice that were boring through the trouts' skin and feasting on their flesh. The sea lice were breeding near newly installed salmon farms in the inlet fed by his river. By the time the salmon farmers started dosing their pens with anti-sea-lice chemicals, the sea-trout fisheries of the west of Ireland were effectively dead. "Sea-trout fishing was sustainable and eco-friendly," says Mantle, "but the salmon farms killed it off within a decade."

Terry McCarthy and Campbell River, "Is Fish Farming Safe?"
Time, *November 17, 2002. www.time.com/time/globalbusiness/*
article/0,9171,1101021125-391523,00.html.

2010 the aquaculture industry could well be using all of the world's fish oil and half of its fishmeal.

But small pelagic fish are a finite resource, and many stocks are already fished at—or over—their safe biological limit. A number of fisheries that supply the fish feed industry are located along the coast of Peru and Chile in the southeast Pacific Ocean. In 2001, the United Nations Food and Agriculture Organization (FAO) characterized these fisheries as "fully fished", meaning that they are fished at the maximum safe biological limit. These fish populations also fluctuate under the influence of El Niño events, making them particularly sensitive to overfishing. South American pilchard catches for example, have decreased drastically from 6.5 million tonnes in 1985 to around 60,000 tonnes in 2001 as a result of El Niño and overfishing.

North East Atlantic fisheries, the other main source of industry fish, were characterized as fully fished in 1983, and as overfished in 1994. The species most under threat today is blue whiting (*Micromesistius poutassou*). These fish are harvested outside safe biological limits—the total catch of 1.8 million tonnes in 2001 was more than double the quota recommended by the International Council for the Exploration of the Sea (ICES). ICES scientists fear that if the present fishing effort continues, the stock will collapse. All this adds up to a feed supply crisis for the fish farming industry.

Feeder Fish Stocks Are Over-exploited

"Demand for fish oil by the fish food industry is predicted to exceed available resources within the next decade," says Maren Esmark, Marine Conservation Officer at WWF-Norway, and co-author of a new report on the fish feed industry. "There is no possibility of sustainably increasing catches in any of the southeast Pacific Ocean fisheries. The situation is no better in the North East Atlantic, where many stocks are already overexploited."

It will also be hard to increase the percentage of the catch used for fish oil and fishmeal. Peru and Chile have large human populations and for food-security reasons, both governments advocate the use of fish for human consumption. The

EU [European Union] also forbids the catching of some fish for making fish oil or fishmeal.

Damaging Ecosystems

Collapse of small pelagic fish stocks is not only a problem for fish farms. The fish species used for fishmeal and fish oil are vital for the marine ecosystem. These fish are prey for other fish, birds, and mammals. Heavy exploitation means less food for cod, haddock, and tuna—all commercially important fish—not to mention seabirds such as puffins and marine mammals such as orcas. The irony is that fish farming is widely viewed—and marketed—as a way to take pressure off wild fish.

"Aquaculture can play an important role in providing an adequate supply of fish to consumers," says Dr Simon Cripps, Director of WWF's Endangered Seas Programme. "But at present, the practice of using fishmeal and fish oil derived from wild-caught fish means that instead of relieving pressure, fish farming is contributing to an increased pressure on already threatened fish stocks."

Sustainable fisheries are possible. Some stocks of Atlantic herring collapsed in the 1960s and 70s but recovered after reduced catches and effective management measures were implemented. Blue whiting stocks in the North East Atlantic are under threat largely because there is no international agreement on the management of this species, and the scientific advice from ICES has not been followed. Improved management would obviously help save these stocks.

Problematic Solutions

There are also alternatives to using wild pelagic fish for fish oil and fishmeal. Increased use of offal from fish caught for human consumption is one potential solution that, for the large part, is currently being wasted. Recent years have seen a trend towards processing fish at sea instead of on land. The result is that vast amounts of fish offal are dumped into the ocean. This offal could, however, be used by the fish feed industry.

The fish farming industry is also looking at non-fish sources of feed. One alternative is to increase the use of vegetable proteins. There are several examples where fishmeal and fish oil can be substantially replaced by alternative protein and oil sources.

But the alternatives have their own problems. Offal from fish higher up the food chain is often too contaminated by dioxins and other chemicals to be used directly. Cleaning is possible, but would raise the price of the fish oil and fishmeal. Not all farmed fish can be fed a completely vegetarian diet. In addition, the harvesting of another suggested feed alternative, krill, could seriously affect the marine ecosystem because krill is an integral part of the food chain.

Whatever solution the fish farm industry finds, it must be sustainable and not adversely affect the environment. "The fish farming industry needs to recognise its dependence on natural ecosystems," says Maren Esmark. "Fish used as feed by the industry might be small and not very pretty, but they are an essential part of the marine ecosystem. Farmed fish need to be produced as part of a healthy marine ecosystem, not at its expense. This is the only way that fish farming will ever be sustainable."

Periodical Bibliography

The following articles have been selected to supplement the diverse views presented in this chapter.

BioCycle	"Can Organic Farming Feed Us All, Asks Trade Publication," January 2007.
Frank Bures	"Wild About Organic," *Utne*, November/ December 2006.
Phillip Clarke	"Ten Years On: World Divided Over Benefits of GM Crop Production," *Farmers Weekly*, October 14, 2005.
Gerald D. Coleman	"Is Genetic Engineering the Answer to Hunger?" *America*, February 21, 2005.
Osha Gray Davidson	"The Farmer Goes to the Sea," *Popular Science*, April 2006.
Economist	"Ethical Food: Good Food?" December 9, 2006.
Julian Gairdner	"Organic Opportunity," *Farmers Weekly*, August 18, 2006.
Paul Greenberg	"Green to the Gills," *New York Times Magazine*, June 18, 2006.
Alana Herro	"Eye on Earth," *World Watch*, January/February 2007.
Karen Hopkin	"The Risks on the Table," *Scientific American Special Edition*, December 2006.
Unmesh Kher, Kristina Dell, & Kathleen Kingsbury	"Oceans of Nothing," *Time*, November 13, 2006.
Sean McDonagh	"Genetic Engineering Is Not the Answer," *America*, May 2, 2005.
Arlene Weintraub	"Online Extra: Salmon that Grow Up Fast," *Business Week Online*, January 11, 2006.

CHAPTER 3

What Alternative Energy Sources Are Worth Pursuing?

Chapter Preface

In a March 2005 article in the *International Herald Tribune*, Donald J. Johnston begins an editorial by stating, "Global energy demand is rising dramatically, particularly in developing countries. Over the next few years, China and India will develop significant nuclear capacity. Smaller developing countries will follow suit. They have to, if they are to respond to the energy needs of their citizens." Johnston goes on to explain why he believes nuclear power will be a major player among the various energy resources needed to fuel the future.

> Certainly, biomass, wind power, hydro power and solar panels can help. But the contribution of these sources of energy to the world's energy needs is predicted to remain modest: 14 percent at most. Nuclear is at present the only viable proven technology that can meet rising energy demand without producing the greenhouse gases that threaten the future of our planet.

Despite nuclear power's non-carbon-producing benefits, Johnston acknowledges that it is not a risk-free energy source. He maintains, though, that governments have and can continue to monitor facilities for potential reactor problems and can ensure the safe disposal of spent nuclear waste. Since he advocates nuclear power as a global remedy for energy concerns in the future, he suggests the creation of an international monitoring association that can handle problems with worldwide ramifications.

Such an optimistic view of nuclear power is not shared by all energy researchers or policymakers. Sidestepping the glaring problems of nuclear waste and potential nuclear meltdown, the Nuclear Information & Resource Service (NIRS) argues that converting to nuclear power would not solve the problems associated with greenhouse gases and climate change. The organization points out that the construction of nuclear plants as well as the mining of uranium fuel would require a large expenditure of carbon emissions, an amount that would be compounded by the numerous plants that would have to be built to supply the world's energy. The NIRS states:

> To reduce the emissions of the public energy sector according to the targets of the Kyoto Protocol [an international agreement to reduce carbon emissions worldwide], 72 new medium-sized nuclear plants would be required in the 15 current European nations. These would have to be built before the end of the first [Kyoto] commitment period: 2008–2012. Leaving aside the huge costs this would involve, it is unlikely that it is technically feasible to build so many new plants in such a short time, given that only 15 new reactors have been built in the last 20 years. In the U.S, as many as 1,000 new reactors would be required—none have been successfully ordered since 1973.

The NIRS fears that such a large undertaking would divert energy and resources away from more feasible plans to reduce fossil fuel dependency.

The authors in Chapter 3 examine other alternative energy sources that, unlike nuclear power, are considered more environmentally friendly because they purportedly create no waste and do not pose hazardous risks. Some see these alternatives as viable means to avoid a fossil fuel crisis; others view them as idealistic fantasies that could never deliver the power needed to drive the modern world.

"*Solar electric systems are some of the most reliable products available today.*"

Solar Energy Can Effectively Provide Electricity

National Renewable Energy Laboratory

In the following viewpoint, researchers at the National Renewable Energy Laboratory (NREL) dispel what they describe as myths surrounding solar energy. They claim that research shows that solar energy is a clean and reliable source of electricity that is used effectively now and has an even more promising future. The National Renewable Energy Laboratory is the nation's primary laboratory for renewable energy and energy efficiency research and development.

As you read, consider the following questions:

1. According to the article, what percent of America's current electricity needs could be supplied with solar electric systems built on abandoned industrial sites?

2. What are some of the ways in which solar electric systems are currently used?

National Renewable Energy Laboratory, "Myths About Solar Electricity," January 2003. http://www.nrel.gov/docs/fy03osti/32529.pdf.

3. What do researchers believe the future holds for solar energy technology?

Solar electric systems are an important part of the whole-building approach to constructing a better home or commercial building. Although these systems have delivered clean, reliable power for more than a decade, several myths have evolved that confuse the real issues of using solar electricity effectively.

Solar Electricity Can Meet High Demands

Myth #1: Solar electricity cannot contribute a significant fraction of the nation's electricity needs.

Solar electric panels can meet electricity demand on any scale, from a single home to a large city. There is plenty of energy in the sunlight shining on all parts of our nation to generate the electricity we need. For example, with today's commercial systems, the solar energy resource in a 100-by-100-mile area of Nevada could supply the United States with all of its electricity. If these systems were distributed to the 50 states, the land required from each state would be an area of about 17 by 17 miles. This area is available now from parking lots, rooftops, and vacant land. In fact, 90% of America's current electricity needs could be supplied with solar electric systems built on the estimated 5 million acres of abandoned industrial sites in our nation's cities.

Solar Electricity Will Improve As Time Goes On

Myth #2: Solar electricity can do everything—right now!

Solar electricity will eventually contribute a significant part of our electricity supply, but the industry required to produce these systems must grow more than tenfold over the next 10 years. In 2001, about 400 megawatts of solar electric modules were produced worldwide. According to an industry-planning document, in order to supply just 10% of U.S. generation capacity by 2030, the U.S. solar electricity industry must supply more than 3,200 megawatts per year. Most experts agree that with continued research, solar electric systems will become more efficient, even more reliable, and less expensive.

Solar Electric Systems Produce Clear Electricity

Myth #3: Producing solar electric systems creates pollution and uses more energy than the system can produce over its lifetime.

Producing solar electric systems uses energy and produces some unwanted byproducts. However, most solar electric systems pay back the energy used to produce them in about one year. Because the systems generally last 30 years, during the 30 years of a system's life, it is producing free and clean electricity for 29 of those years.

Production of solar electric systems is regulated by rigorous safety and pollution control standards. In addition, during the lifetime of a solar electric system, pollution that would have been emitted by conventional generation of electricity is avoided. For each kilowatt of solar electric generating capacity, the pollution avoided by not using fossil fuels to produce electricity amounts to 9 kilograms of sulfuric oxide, 16 kilograms of nitrous oxide, and between 600 and 2,300 kilograms of carbon dioxide per year. The annual amount of carbon dioxide offset by a 2.5-kW rooftop residential solar electric system is equal to that emitted by a typical family car during that same year.

Solar Electricity Has Multiple Applications

Myth #4: Solar electric systems make sense in only a few applications.

Solar electric systems make sense nearly anywhere electricity is needed. Homes and businesses that are already using

125

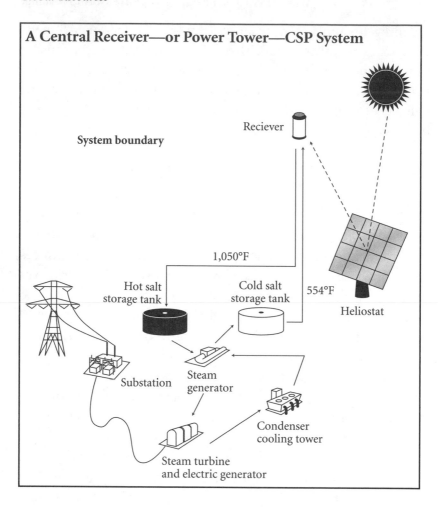

A Central Receiver—or Power Tower—CSP System

System boundary

Reciever

1,050°F

Hot salt storage tank

Cold salt storage tank

554°F

Heliostat

Substation

Steam generator

Condenser cooling tower

Steam turbine and electric generator

electricity from the utility . . . represent nearly 60% of the market for solar electric systems. The number of these grid-connected applications is growing because they make sense economically, environmentally, and aesthetically. Solar electric systems make economic sense because they use free fuel from the sun and require little upkeep because they have no moving parts. Every bit of electricity produced is used in the home or sold back to the electric utility for use by other customers. Solar electric systems also make sense for the environment and can blend seamlessly into the design of a building.

Solar Electricity Is Reliable

Myth #5: Solar electric systems are unreliable and produce substandard electricity.

Solar electric systems are some of the most reliable products available today. They are silent, have no moving parts, and have been tested to rigorous standards by public and private organizations. Many solar electric products have been tested and listed by Underwriters Laboratories, just as electrical appliances are. Warranties of 20–25 years are standard for most modules.

Solar electric systems connected to the utility grid generate the same kind of power as that from the power line. Today's systems must meet the requirements of the National Electrical Code, the local utility, and local building codes. Once these systems are installed according to these requirements, the owner of a solar-electric-powered home has electricity of the same quality as any other utility customer....

The Future of Solar Electricity Is Bright

In the future, people will reflect on our current solar electric technology much as we reflect on the technology of the Model T Ford: with admiration for the pioneering visionaries of the day and perhaps amusement at the technology that seems so primitive compared to what we now enjoy. Researchers believe that in the future, new physics and technologies will be developed that will greatly improve solar energy technology. As for the present day, clean, reliable solar electricity is increasingly popular with home and business owners, which helps to dispel the myths surrounding this technology.

"If there were large energy-producing facilities in the [U.S.] deserts, how would the energy be delivered to New York, Boston, Washington, D.C., Philadelphia, Atlanta, and Chicago, thousands of kilometers distant?"

Solar Energy Is Inefficient and Impractical

Howard C. Hayden

In this viewpoint, Howard C. Hayden argues that solar energy is too expensive and difficult to produce in quantities necessary to power the world. According to Hayden, solar collection facilities currently can produce only an insignificant fraction of the world's energy needs and would have to be increased to titanic proportions to make a dent in those needs. Even then, he maintains, it would be difficult to transport the energy any great distance from these installations. The alternative of equipping every home, office building, and industrial facility with its own set of solar collecting cells would also be doomed to failure because of the roof space required to gather enough sunlight, Hayden asserts. Howard C. Hayden is an emeritus professor of physics at the University of Connecticut.

Howard C. Hayden, *The Solar Fraud: Why Solar Energy Won't Run the World*, Vales Lake Publishing, LLC, 2004, pp. 181–207. Copyright © 2004 by Vales Lake Publishing, LLC. All rights reserved. Reproduced by permission.

As you read, consider the following questions:

1. In Hayden's view, how many square miles of land would be needed for a Solar-Two installation to generate as much power as a typical 1,000-MWe (megawatt electrical) power plant does?

2. What are some of the problems Hayden mentions concerning the placement of solar cells on rooftops to supply power for residential and business use?

3. How efficient are most solar cells that are large enough for solar applications?

There is nothing particularly new about the concept of converting sunlight to electricity. In 1822, T. S. Seebeck obtained an electric current by heating one of the junctions of a bi-metallic ring, and it was only a matter of time before thermocouples using the Seebeck effect were in use as temperature-measuring devices. Let the source of heat be sunlight, and there's solar electricity, albeit of low efficiency.

Another way to use sunlight to produce electricity is to focus the sun's rays to heat water (directly or indirectly) to a high enough temperature to run a steam engine.

Yet a third way, discovered in 1878, but commercially developed within the last few decades, is to produce electricity directly, without having to produce heat. Everybody these days is familiar with solar-powered calculators, for example. It is this new, somewhat exotic, *photovoltaic* technology that has some people very excited about solar energy for the future. In the view of some, it is an infant technology that will eventually become cheap enough to enjoy widespread use. After all, solar cells are made of silicon, the same stuff that computer chips are made of. "Look how the price has been dropping!" they say. Don't count on it.

Problems with Large Solar Installations

There are two major installations in the US devoted to producing electricity from the heat of sunlight. Of course, sunlight has to be concentrated to produce the high temperatures necessary. The installation at Solar Two near Barstow, California, shows one method to accomplish the task, and the parabolic-trough array at Daggett, California, shows another. Both installations are in the best solar location in the US, namely, the Mojave Desert.

In a unit called *Solar Two*, computer-controlled mirrors reflect light onto a central tower where the concentrated sunlight heats a heat-transfer oil called *therminol*. The hot therminol is pumped to a heat exchanger where the heat is transferred to water to make steam to run an engine. The engine is coupled to a generator to produce electricity.

It is important to understand that magnifying glasses and mirrors *concentrate* light, but *do not create it*. We all learned, as children, how to cause high temperature by focusing the sun's rays into one bright spot. . . .

In the Solar Two installation, the distance to the farthest mirror is about four times the height of the tower. . . . Obviously, the mirrors need to be spread out considerably so as to avoid the shading problem.

Solar Two is, of course, a demonstration project that is not intended to provide serious amounts of power. But how could it be scaled up? One way would be to double the diameter of the field of mirrors and to double the height of the tower. The mirrors would quadruple the power delivered to the top of the tower. Of course, the tower would have to be twice as tall [to avoid problems with more distant rows of mirrors shading subsequent rows] and would have to carry the additional weight of the larger power-handling equipment. The legs would have to be *more* than four times as strong, not only to carry the additional load, but to provide more rigidity against wind thrust. All in all, then, there is little point in increasing the size. It would probably be just as easy to simply build another entire system, tower, mirrors, and all.

The Solar Two site occupies 52.6 hectares (130 acres) and produces 10 MWe [megawatt electrical] *peak*. Its capacity factor is about 16%. For a Solar-Two installation to produce as much energy as a typical 1000-MWe power plant does in a year, it would have to cover about 33,000 hectares (127 square miles). That is environmental impact! . . .

Not far away from Solar Two, in Kramer Junction, California, there is another solar installation called *SEGS* (Solar Electric Generating System, built by LUZ International), of which there are nine units, SEGS uses an array of parabolic mirrors, laid out on north-south axes to concentrate reflected sunlight onto a black tube through which therminol flows. The therminol delivers the heat to a Rankine steam engine whose shaft turns a generator. The SEGS installation has a natural gas boiler and a gas reheater. The purpose of the gas assist is to assure that the steam turbine receives steam at 371°C regardless of the actual temperature of the therminol in the solar field.

Together, the nine SEGS units have about 2.3 million square meters of "aperture," the cross-sectional area of the mirror assembly facing upwards. At a full summer noontime intensity of about 950 watts per square meter, the system is exposed to about 2.2 billion watts of solar heat. . . .

According to the National Renewable Energy Lab (NREL), the productivity of the SEGS system is about 0.5 MWe/hectare (equal to 50 W/m²), referring to *peak* MWe per unit of land area. With the capacity factor of 22%, this amounts to an around-the-clock average of about 10.8 watts per square meter. To scale that up to the size of a 1000-MWe plant would require 92 square kilometers, or about 33 square miles. . . .

Difficulties of Distance

The best place in the US for solar collectors of any sort is the desert Southwest, if we ignore the difficulties in transmitting power to other parts of the nation. That is, of course, why

Solar Power Drawbacks, cartoon. Copyright © 2006 by Patrick Corrigan and Caglecartoons.com. All rights reserved.

both Solar-Two and the SEGS units are in the Mojave Desert. [In their 1991 book, *Saving the Planet: How to Shape an Environmentally Sustainable Global Economy*, Lester] Brown, [Christopher] Flavin, [and Sandra] Postel discuss putting huge solar collectors in the desert, and shortly thereafter say, "Decentralization may be another hallmark of the emerging new energy system."

With respect to "decentralization," there is little to distinguish large companies producing energy in the desert environment from large companies producing energy by some other means elsewhere.

If there were large energy-producing facilities in the deserts, how would the energy be delivered to New York, Boston, Washington, D.C., Philadelphia, Atlanta, and Chicago, thousands of kilometers distant? High-voltage power lines? Through whose neighborhood?

Not Enough Roof Space

"Solar technologies need not be spread over large swaths of land. Photovoltaics can be deployed on rooftops."

Brown, Flavin & Postel (1991)

There are about 100 million homes in the United States. For the sake of argument, let us assume that every one of them occupies 150 square meters of land area. That amounts to 15 billion square meters. Hypothetically, if *every* roof were fully covered with solar cells at 10% efficiency, every square meter could generate a year-round average of 20 watts per square meter. That amounts to 300 GW_e [Gigawatts electrical].

Life isn't that simple. Apartment dwellers have virtually no roof area available to themselves. Houses usually have a roofline that extends north-south or east-west. The houses best suited to solar collectors are those with a southern exposure.

But there are more problems. Most houses are in cities or suburbs. A characteristic of people in such places is to plant trees, often deliberately on the south side of the house to shade the house in summer. In the largely treeless west, you can spot towns miles away simply because they have trees.

All things considered, rooftops on American homes might be able to generate a year-round average of about 10 to 20 GW_e. Even that possibility is entirely hypothetical, of course. Most people cannot afford to cover even part, let alone the entire south-facing roof with solar collectors.

In fact, photovoltaic arrays are being put on rooftops, mostly courtesy of taxpayers. For example, a new 127-kW (peak) photovoltaic array has been installed on the roof of a U.S. Postal Service processing plant 11 miles southwest of downtown Los Angeles. The array is the size of a football field. Winston Hickox, secretary of the state Environmental Protection Agency cooed, "Relying on solar energy is no longer just a feel-good endeavor."

And how good is this beauty? It will provide a whopping 10% of the facility's electricity during peak hours, when there is the least need for interior lighting. A ten-football-field area could provide 100% of the power during peak hours. Fifty or sixty football fields' worth of PV could provide enough energy around the clock—if they had a 100%-efficient storage and retrieval system.

With generous subsidies from both the federal government and the state government, the system cost the post office only $225,000. That amounts to $1.77 per installed peak watt and about $10 per installed average watt.

Admitting Failure

The Swiss government "regrets the early end of the solar photovoltaic subsidy program," that had "resulted in 378 installations across Switzerland". All together, the PV installations produce a whopping 3,660 megawatt-hours of electricity annually, about as much as a nuke produces during the playing of one football game.

The Swiss plan, of course, was to increase the contribution of renewables to the overall energy supply. "The overall goal of the wider program, which started in 1990, was to increase renewable energy usage by 0.5% over 10 years. In fact, an increase of 0.7% was achieved, with significant contributions coming from wood and biomass," says *Newsbuzz* without saying *how much* of the contribution actually came from highly vaunted photovoltaics.

Switzerland generates about 67 million megawatt-hours per year, so the annual 3,660 megawatt-hours is a piddling 0.0005 percent of the total. Said another way, if they subsidized 6.9 million PV installations instead of the mere 378, they could produce as much energy from PV as they do from their conventional power sources. That is, if they had a method to store the energy. . . .

Elusive Photovoltaic Efficiency

Solar cells that are large enough to be useful for solar applications are about 10% efficient. Small experimental PV cells made of exotic materials have achieved much higher efficiencies, some in the range of 20%. It is to be hoped that high efficiency can be obtained for solar cells that can be mass-produced so that large areas can be covered cheaply.

The primary method of attack is to make the PV cell in layers. The layer facing the sun uses blue light, but is transparent to all other colors. The next layer down absorbs green light and is transparent to all longer wavelengths, and so on. Everything is engineered so that if a given amount of sunlight causes a million transitions in the "blue" layer, it will also cause a million transitions in each other layer. The current must be the same in all layers, and will be limited by the current in the weakest layer.

This Holy Grail of photovoltaics has remained elusive. Be reminded that the most democratic institution on earth is the periodic table, found in classrooms throughout the world. This list contains the elements—*all* of them—that exist for constructing PV cells (or anything else). The reward for developing reliable, inexpensive, high-efficiency PV cells will easily be in the billions of dollars, as everybody has recognized from the outset. Still, despite many decades of corporate and university research, such PV cells have not been developed.

"*If environmental, social, and human-health costs were reflected in the economics of electricity generation, wind energy would become even less costly compared to energy derived from fossil fuels.*"

Wind Power Is Affordable and Environmentally Friendly

Joseph Florence

Joseph Florence was a research associate for the Earth Policy Institute, a research organization devoted to ensuring an environmentally sustainable economy. In this viewpoint, Florence describes the expansion of wind power usage across the globe. The growth in wind energy investment, Florence contends, is partly due to ever-improving technology and falling costs of turbine construction. It is also an attractive energy source because it is environmentally friendly and not subject to unstable market prices, Florence adds.

Joseph Florence, "Global Wind Power Expands in 2006," *Eco-Economy Indicator* (Washington, D.C.: Earth Policy Institute, June 28, 2006). Copyright © 2006 Earth Policy Institute. Reproduced by permission.

As you read, consider the following questions:

1. As Florence notes, what percentage of European electricity needs is the European Wind Energy Association hoping to satisfy with wind power by 2030?

2. How many megawatts of wind power did the United States wind industry install in 2005, as Florence reports?

3. According to Florence, what accounts for the largest part of wind energy costs?

Global wind electricity-generating capacity increased by 24 percent in 2005 to 59,100 megawatts. This represents a twelvefold increase from a decade ago, when world wind-generating capacity stood at less than 5,000 megawatts. Wind is the world's fastest-growing energy source with an average annual growth rate of 29 percent over the last ten years. In contrast, over the same time period, coal use has grown by 2.5 percent per year, nuclear power by 1.8 percent, natural gas by 2.5 percent, and oil by 1.7 percent.

Europe continues to lead the world in total installed capacity with over 40,500 megawatts, or two-thirds of the global total. These wind installations supply nearly 3 percent of Europe's electricity and produce enough power to meet the needs of over 40 million people. The European Wind Energy Association (EWEA) has set a target to satisfy 23 percent of European electricity needs with wind by 2030. EWEA also notes that Europe has enough wind resources to meet the electricity demands of all of its countries.

Wind Power Capacity in Europe and the United States

Germany, the country with the most installed wind-generating capacity, now gets 6 percent of its electricity from its 18,400 megawatts of wind power. Spain, in second place with over 10,000 megawatts of capacity, gets 8 percent of its electricity from wind.

Denmark's 3,100 megawatts of wind capacity meet 20 percent of its electricity needs, the largest share in any country. It ranks fifth in the world in installed capacity. Denmark is also the global leader in offshore wind power installations, with 400 megawatts of existing capacity. Globally, over 900 megawatts of offshore wind capacity will be installed by the end of 2006, all in Europe.

The U.S. has installed 9,100 megawatts of wind power capacity. The U.S. wind industry installed a record-breaking 2,400 megawatts of wind power in 2005, up from installing just 370 megawatts in 2004 and 1,700 megawatts in 2003. This inconsistent growth is mostly due to the intermittent availability of the federal wind production tax credit (PTC) that currently stands at 1.9¢ per kilowatt hour. In mid 2005, Congress extended the PTC by two years, marking the first time lawmakers extended the tax credit without first allowing it to lapse. With the PTC guaranteed for the year, the U.S. wind industry projects that it will install 25 percent more capacity in 2006 than it did in 2005.

Wind Power Capacity in Canada, Asia, and Other Regions

Canada's installed wind capacity of 680 megawatts at the end of 2005 is expected to increase to 1,200 megawatts by the end of 2006. While Canada's federal government targets the installation of 4,000 megawatts of wind energy by 2010, its more ambitious provincial governments plan to install a combined 9,200 megawatts by 2015.

Asian countries have installed nearly 7,000 megawatts of wind-generated electricity capacity. India has 4,400 megawatts of capacity, ranking fourth after Germany, the United States, and Spain. Wind power in China, currently at 1,260 mega-

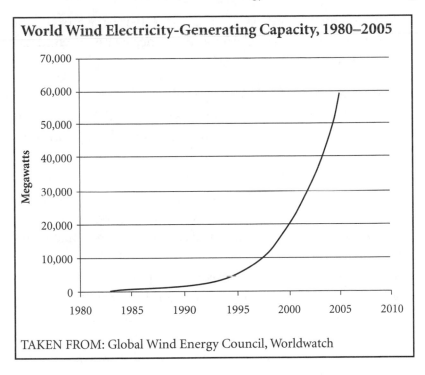

World Wind Electricity-Generating Capacity, 1980–2005

TAKEN FROM: Global Wind Energy Council, Worldwatch

watts, is beginning to flourish due to the country's new Renewable Energy Law. This law provides tax incentives and subsidies for wind power and targets the development of 30,000 megawatts of wind capacity by 2010. Ambitious as these goals are, experts within the Chinese wind industry report that China could produce 400,000 megawatts of wind capacity by 2050. For comparison, China's total electric power generation capacity at the end of 2003 was 356,100 megawatts.

While three-quarters of all wind power has been installed in only five countries, the wind power installed in the rest of the world has grown by an average of 35 percent per year over the past ten years. Australia's wind capacity almost doubled in 2005 to 710 megawatts. It leads the countries of the Pacific region, which, as a whole, have developed 890 megawatts. Latin America and the Caribbean have installed 210 megawatts of capacity. North African countries are also beginning to develop wind power and have installed 310 megawatts. Egypt and Morocco have installed 150 and 60 megawatts of wind capacity, respectively.

Decreasing Costs of Wind Power

Overall, the cost of wind power has decreased by nearly 90 percent since the 1980s to 4¢ or less per kilowatt-hour in prime wind sites. In some markets wind-generated electricity is cheaper than electricity from conventional energy sources. The cost of wind power has fallen due to advances in technology, declines in the costs of financing wind projects, and the economies of scale of turbine and component manufacturing and construction.

The explosive growth of world wind power is due in large part to its increasing technological sophistication. Modern turbines are taller and have longer rotor blades than the turbines of 20 years ago, allowing them to produce up to 200 times more power. Since the "fuel" for wind power is free and unlimited, 75 to 90 percent of the costs of generating electricity with wind lie in manufacturing and constructing wind turbines and connecting them to the grid. Once turbines are installed, the remaining costs are primarily turbine operation and maintenance, land-use royalties, and property taxes.

In the United States and around the world, energy markets are heavily regulated. Some 48 countries have regulations or laws in place that favor the growth of renewable energies. Examples of these include renewable portfolio standards that set a minimum for renewable energy purchases and tax incentives such as the United States' PTC. However, decades of political and financial support to fossil fuel industries often undermine the competitiveness of wind energy.

Environmental and Other Benefits of Wind Power

If environmental, social, and human-health costs were reflected in the economics of electricity generation, wind energy would become even less costly compared to energy derived from fossil fuels. Unlike conventional power plants, wind electrical generation does not release greenhouse gases that warm the climate or other polluting emissions.

Wind power provides more benefits than just affordable clean energy. The prices of wind-generated electricity are stable and not subject to the price volatility of fossil fuels. Wind power supports local economic development since the jobs, royalties, and tax revenues from wind-generated electricity production tend to stay in the community. And since wind is inexhaustible it offers long-term energy security that electricity derived from nonrenewable fossil fuels cannot.

> "Even the small benefits claimed by [wind power] promoters are far out-stripped by the huge negative impacts."

Wind Power Is Unreliable and Not Environmentally Friendly

Eric Rosenbloom

In this viewpoint, Eric Rosenbloom, a writer and science editor living in Vermont, argues that wind power is not a practical solution to global energy needs. According to Rosenbloom, countries that have tried to adopt wind energy on a grand scale have failed to reduce their reliance on conventional power facilities. This is mainly due to the unreliability of the wind to blow hard enough and long enough to sustain the needed power supply. Rosenbloom also asserts that wind power is not as environmentally friendly as it is assumed because wind turbines create noise and visual clutter and damage environments where they are located.

As you read, consider the following questions:

1. As Rosenbloom notes, what was the percentage of electrical output of all the wind turbines in Denmark in February 2003?

Eric Rosenbloom, "A Problem With Wind Power," *American Wind Energy Opposition*, September 5, 2006. Reproduced by permission.

2. What kinds of animals have been negatively impacted by giant wind turbines?

3. What does Rosenbloom suggest would have a significant impact on pollution and foreign-oil dependence?

Wind power promises a clean and free source of electricity, it will reduce our dependence on imported fossil fuels and reduce the output of greenhouse gases and other pollution. Many governments are therefore promoting the construction of vast wind "farms," encouraging private companies with generous subsidies and regulatory support, requiring utilities to buy from them, and setting up markets for the trade of "green credits" in addition to actual energy. The U.S. Department of Energy (DOE) aims to see 5% of our electricity produced by wind turbine in 2010. Energy companies are eagerly investing in wind power, finding the arrangement quite profitable.

A little research, however, reveals that wind power does not in fact live up to the claims made by its advocates (see part I), that its impact on the environment and people's lives is far from benign (see part II), and that with such a poor record and prospect the money spent on it could be much more effectively directed (see part III).

Part I: Wind Power Is Not Making Good on Its Promises

In 1998, Norway commissioned a study of wind power in Denmark and concluded that it has "serious environmental effects, insufficient production, and high production costs."

Denmark (population 5.3 million) has over 6,000 turbines that produced electricity equal to 19% of what the country used in 2002. Yet no conventional power plant has been shut down. Because of the intermittency and variability of the wind, conventional power plants must be kept running at full capacity to meet the actual demand for electricity. Most cannot simply be turned on and off as the wind dies and rises, and the quick ramping up and down of those that can be would actually increase their output of pollution and carbon dioxide (CO_2, the primary "greenhouse" gas). So when the wind is blowing just right for the turbines, the power they generate is usually a surplus and sold to other countries at an extremely discounted price, or the turbines must be shut off.

A writer in *The Utilities Journal* (David J. White, "Danish Wind: Too Good To Be True?," July 2004) found that 84% of western Denmark's wind-generated electricity was exported (at a revenue loss) in 2003, i.e., Denmark's glut of wind towers provided only 3.3% of the nation's electricity. According to *The Wall Street Journal Europe*, the Copenhagen newspaper *Politiken* reported that wind actually met only 1.7% of Denmark's total demand in 1999. Besides the amount exported, this low figure may also reflect the actual *net* contribution. The large amount of electricity used by the turbines themselves is typically not accounted for in the usually cited output figures. In *Weekendavisen* (Nov. 4, 2005), Frede Vestergaard reported that Denmark as a whole exported 70.3% of its wind production in 2004.

Denmark is just dependent enough on wind power that when the wind is not blowing right they must import electricity. In 2000 they imported more electricity than they exported. And added to the Danish electric bill are the subsidies that support the private companies building the wind towers. Danish electricity costs for the consumer are the highest in Europe.

The head of Xcel Energy in the U.S., Wayne Brunetti, has said, "We're a big supporter of wind, but at the time when customers have the greatest needs, it's typically not available." Throughout Europe, wind turbines produced on average less than 20% of their theoretical (or *rated*) capacity. Yet both the British and the American Wind Energy Associations (BWEA

A Misplaced Faith in Wind Power

It is understandably comforting to believe that there is a benign source of electricity that will help to remedy our energy problems. And since most people have not been personally threatened by wind power development, they have little compulsion to question their faith. The belief is reinforced as governments are compelled to reduce fuel imports or carbon emissions. The huge size of industrial wind turbines makes them powerful symbols. Environmental groups thus find themselves in the unusual position of supporting the government and industry and helping to whitewash the negative impacts.

National Wind Watch, "FAQ: The Grid"
www.wind-watch.org.

and AWEA) plan for 30%. The figure in Denmark was 16.8% in 2002 and 19% in 2003 (in February 2003, the output of the more than 6,000 turbines in Denmark was 0!). . . .

Part II: An Unfriendly Energy

In Vermont, billboards are banned from the highways, and development—especially at sites above 2,500 feet—is subject to strong environmental laws, yet many who call themselves environmentalists absurdly support the installation of wind farms on our mountain ridge lines as a desirable trade-off, ignoring wind's dismal record as described in part I.

Even if one thinks that jumbo-jet-sized wind towers dominating every ridge line in sight like a giant barbed-wire fence is a beautiful thing, many people are drawn to wild places to avoid such reminders of human industrial might. Many communities depend on such tourists, who will now seek some other—as yet unspoiled—retreat.

Death of Birds, Bats, and Other Wildlife

The spinning blades kill and maim birds and bats. . . . Wildlife on the ground is displaced as well. Prairie birds are especially affected by disturbance of their habitat, and construction on mountain ridges diminishes important forest interior far beyond the extent of the clearing itself. A visitor to the Backbone Mountain facility wrote, "I looked around me, to a place where months before had been prime country for deer, wild turkey, and yes, black bear, to see positively no sign of any of the animals about at all. This alarmed me, so I scouted in the woods that afternoon. All afternoon, I found no sign, sight, or peek of any animal about."

Noise

The same West Virginia writer found the noise from the turbines on Backbone Mountain to be "incredible. It surprised me. It sounded like airplanes or helicopters. And it traveled. Sometimes, you could not hear the sound standing right under one, but you heard it 3,000 yards down the hill." Yet the industry insists such noise is a thing of the past. Indeed, new turbines may have quieter bearings and gears, but the huge magnetized generators can not avoid producing a low-frequency hum, and the problem of 100-foot rotor blades chopping through the air at over 100 mph also is insurmountable (a 35-meter [115-foot] blade turning at 15 rpm is travelling 123 mph at the tip, at 20 rpm 164 mph). Every time each rotor passes the tower, the compression of air produces a deep resonating thump. Only a gravelly "swishing" may be heard directly beneath the turbine, but farther away the resulting sound of several towers together has been described to be as loud as a motorcycle, like aircraft continually passing overhead, a "brick wrapped in a towel turning in a tumble dryer," "as if someone was mixing cement in the sky," "like a train that never arrives." It is a relentless rumble like unceasing thunder from an approaching storm. . . .

Part III: Better Use of Finances

It is wise to diversify the sources of our energy. But the money and legislative effort invested in large-scale wind generation could be spent much more effectively to achieve the goal of reducing our use of fossil and nuclear fuels.

As an example, Country Guardian calculates that for the U.K. government subsidy towards the construction of one wind turbine, they could insulate the roofs of almost 500 houses that need it and save in two years the amount of energy the wind turbine might produce over its lifetime.

Country Guardian also calculates that if every light bulb in the U.K. were switched to a more efficient one, the country could shut down an entire power plant—something even Denmark, with wind producing as much as 20% of their electricity, is not able to do. According to solar energy consultant and retailer Real Goods, if every household in the U.S. replaced one incandescent bulb with a compact fluorescent bulb, one nuclear power plant could be closed. . . .

As described in part I, wind farms do not bring about any reduction in the use of conventional power plants. Requiring the upgrading of power plants to be more efficient and cleaner would actually do something rather than simply support the image of "green" power that energy companies profit from while in fact doing nothing to reduce pollution or fuel imports. . . .

Despite the manic installation of wind facilities in the U.K., their CO_2 emissions rose in 2002 and 2003. At a May 27, 2004, conference in Copenhagen, the head of development from the Danish energy company Elsam stated, "Increased development of wind turbines does not reduce Danish CO_2 emissions." Demanding better gas mileage in cars, including pickup trucks and SUVs, promoting rail for both freight and travel, and supporting the use of biodiesel (for example, from hemp) would make a huge impact on pollution and dependence on foreign oil, whereas wind power makes none. . . .

Wind Is Not the Solution

On a small scale, where a turbine directly supplies the users and the fluctuating production can be stored, wind can contribute to a home, school, factory, office building, or even small village's electricity. But this simply does not work on a large scale to supply the grid. Even the small benefits claimed by their promoters are far outstripped by the huge negative impacts. . . .

Many alternative sources of energy, as well as dramatic improvements in the use of current sources, are in development. But wind turbines exist, so they are presented by their manufacturers and managers as *the* solution. Every effort is made to maintain the illusion that they are in fact a solution when a few simple questions reveal they are not.

> *"I believe we can replace most of our gasoline needs in 25 years with biomass from our farmlands and municipal waste. ..."*

Biofuels Can Replace Gasoline

Vinod Khosla

In this viewpoint, Vinod Khosla insists that embracing ethanol is the first step in weaning the world off gasoline and shifting dependence to cleaner, cheaper biofuels. Ethanol and other biofuels, Khosla maintains, are easily manufactured from corn crops and animal waste, and the technology to use these fuels already exists. Given the necessary financial and technological investment in biofuels, Khosla expects that America at least could end its reliance on gasoline in a matter of decades. Vinod Khosla is a founder of Sun Microsystems and a partner in Khosla Ventures, an investment firm.

As you read, consider the following questions:

1. How many gallons of fuel per ton of biomass docs Khosla think the United States can produce with the aid of new technologies?

2. As Khosla describes, what factor made the use of ethanol more popular in Brazil in 2003–2004?

3. According to Khosla, how many service stations
   were already offering E85 ethanol fuel in 2006?

It may surprise you to learn that the most promising solution to our nation's energy crisis begins in the bowels of a
waste trough, under the slotted concrete floor of a giant pen
that holds 28,000 Angus, Hereford, and Charolais beef cattle.
But for some time now, I've been searching for a renewable
fuel that could realistically replace the 140 billion gallons of
gasoline consumed in the US each year. And now I believe the
key to producing this fuel starts with cow manure—because
this waste powers a facility that turns corn into ethanol. . . .

The First Step Toward Cheaper, Cleaner Fuels

A company called E3 Biofuels is about to fire up the most
energy-efficient corn ethanol facility in the country: a $75
million state-of the-art biorefinery and feedlot capable of producing 25 million gallons of ethanol a year. What's more, it
will run on methane gas produced from cow manure. The
super-efficient operation capitalizes on a closed loop of resources available here on the prairie—cattle (fed on corn),
manure (from the cows), and corn (fed into the ethanol
distiller). The output: a potential gusher of renewable, energy-
efficient transportation fuel.

Of course, 25 million gallons of ethanol is a drop in the
tanker when it comes to our 140 billion-a-year oil habit. And
ethanol itself is a subject of controversy for all sorts of reasons. Many of the criticisms, while true in some small ways,
are aggressively promoted by the oil lobby and other interested parties in an effort to forestall change. Most are myths.
Challenges certainly exist with ethanol, but none are insurmountable, and—with apologies to Al Gore—the convenient
truth is that corn ethanol is a crucial first step toward kicking
our oil addiction. I believe we can replace most of our gaso-

line needs in 25 years with biomass from our farmlands and municipal waste, while creating a huge economic boom cycle and a cheaper, cleaner fuel for consumers. . . .

The single most critical variable in the biohol [liquid fuel derived from biomass for internal combustion engines] trajectory is the coming rise in the number of gallons of fuel produced per acre. As we migrate from biomass derived from corn to biomass from so-called energy crops like switchgrass and miscanthus, I estimate that biomass yield will reach 20 to 24 tons per acre, a fourfold increase. At the same time, new technologies will enable us to extract more biohols from every ton of biomass, potentially to 110 gallons per ton. The result: We'll be extracting 2,000 to 2,700 gallons of fuel per acre (as opposed to about 400 gallons with today's technology). With better fuels and more-efficient engines improving mileage by about 50 percent, we can safely predict a seven- to tenfold gain in miles driven per acre of land over the next 25 years. Given this biohol trajectory, a future of independence from gasoline becomes not only possible but probable. And the trajectory begins with garden-variety corn ethanol. . . .

Success in Brazil

I became familiar with ethanol in 2003, when a business plan for a startup called BCI (now known as Celunol) crossed my desk. I had begun to look into alternative fuel technologies, but I couldn't get comfortable with the economics of some of the trendy clean-energy technologies like hydrogen fuel cells.

I was impressed with Celunol's technology for producing cellulosic ethanol (made from the cellulose, or "stalk," of a plant rather than the sugar or starch "seed"), but I didn't think the business was commercially viable. Still, I couldn't bring myself to toss out the plan. It sat on a corner of my desk for nearly 18 months while I read everything I could

Advantages of Switchgrass as a Biofuel

Switchgrass and your suburban lawn grasses ... are about as similar as a shopping-mall ficus and an old-growth redwood. Switchgrass is big and it's tough—after a good growing season, it can stand 10 feet high, with stems as thick and strong as hardwood pencils.

But what makes switchgrass bad for barefoot lawns makes it ideal for energy crops: It grows fast, capturing lots of solar energy and turning it into lots of chemical energy—cellulose—that can be liquified, gasified, or burned directly. It also reaches deep into the soil for water, and uses the water it finds very efficiently.

And because it spent millions of years evolving to thrive in climates and growing conditions spanning much of the nation, switchgrass is remarkably adaptable.

Marie Walsh,
"Biofuels from Switchgrass: Greener Energy Pastures,"
Bioenergy Feedstock Information Network.
http://bioenergy.ornl.gov.

about petroleum and its alternatives and what it would take to produce a replacement fuel for gasoline from a renewable resource.

In 2004, I began hearing about the ethanol market in Brazil, where the government had been unsuccessfully promoting ethanol cars. Consumers wanted a car that could use the much cheaper ethanol fuel but were reluctant to get locked into using ethanol only. When a car that offered the choice of either gasoline or ethanol as a fuel was introduced in 2003 by Volkswagen, sales took off, far surpassing expectations. Today, more than 70 percent of new cars sold in Brazil are so-called flex-fuel vehicles, which can run on gas or ethanol; three years ago, less than 4 percent of new cars were flex-fuel vehicles.

Brazil's example made me think that replacing oil in the US was plausible, perhaps even possible. How, I wondered, could the possible be turned into the probable? Naturally, the US market is significantly different from Brazil's. US consumers use six times as much oil as Brazilians per capita. Brazil gets its ethanol from sugarcane, but the US can't grow much sugarcane (which has an exceptionally high energy efficiency) in our climates. Still, considering the technological creativity and capital at our disposal, I felt certain that the most powerful country in the world could achieve something a country with an economy one-eighth our size had successfully embarked on. . . .

Economic, Scientific, and Pragmatic Incentives

When it comes to technology, the best way to change the world is not by revolution but by evolutionary steps. Change must follow from step to step, from innovation to innovation, as technology matures, each step justifying its economic viability and attracting investment. So while ethanol may not be ideal, I'm convinced it's the best first step on the biohol trajectory. Ethanol offers one thing no other oil substitute can: a clear path from where we are to where we hope to be. . . .

Ethanol is the first step on the biohol trajectory for three reasons. The first is economic: Ethanol can be produced and sold cheaper than gasoline. Most ethanol facilities can produce their fuel for about $1 a gallon—almost half the production cost of gasoline. And innovative producers like E3 Biofuels claim to make it for 75 cents a gallon. It's true that American ethanol today benefits from agricultural subsidies for corn farmers. I would like to eliminate ethanol subsidies gradually in conjunction with the removal of tariffs on imported ethanol. For kicks, we might consider removing the substantial direct subsidies to oil, too. Free markets demand level playing fields.

Meanwhile, ethanol at the pump can be relatively cheap. Recently, in Aberdeen, South Dakota, E85—a blend of 85 percent ethanol and 15 percent gasoline—was selling at gas stations for just $1.95 a gallon. Wal-Mart is now considering selling it. Imagine if every Wal-Mart offered $1.99-a-gallon fuel! The switch to cars and trucks that can run on E85 would be relatively economical, too. There are already 6 million such flex-fuel vehicles on the road in the US. It costs a paltry $35 to make a new car capable of handling both ethanol and gasoline.

The second reason is scientific: New breakthroughs make it eminently feasible to scale up ethanol to national and even global proportions. Today, corn yields about 400 gallons of ethanol per acre of cropland. While corn yields will increase over time thanks to genetic modification (a new variety from Monsanto may yield 750 gallons per acre), corn can get us only so far. The real promise for ethanol lies in cellulose, which can be derived from plants like switchgrass and miscanthus, a tropical grass native to southeast Asia. Cellulosic ethanol technology promises to deliver as much as 2,700 gallons per acre by 2030. This is the key to achieving scale, substantially lower costs, and manageable land-use scenarios. Biotechnology, plant breeding, chemical process technologies, synthetic biology, energy crop engineering, systems biology, computational modeling, and new fuel chemistries will all offer tools, approaches, and possibilities for improvement. Failure to use them will be a failure of imagination.

The third reason is pragmatic: Ethanol is already here—and in use! We know how to produce it, we know how to distribute it, and we already have cars that can use it. So why reinvent the wheel? Today in the US [2006], there are 925 stations that dispense E85. Expanding that number to just 20,000 would be sufficient to make E85 broadly available—an investment I estimate at much less than a billion dollars. . . .

Ethanol Is Here

We don't need far-off technologies like hydrogen fuel cells to achieve a future that is more environmentally and economically secure. And we don't have to pay more for cleaner transportation energy. We have the fuel in ethanol, and we have the technology to produce it, the distribution systems to move it, the pumps to dispense it, and the cars to run on it—all in place and ready to go today. The doorway to a future with fewer economic and environmental risks is before us. All we need do is step through it.

> *"It's difficult to understand how advo-*
> *cates of biofuels can believe they are a*
> *real solution to kicking our oil addic-*
> *tion."*

Biofuels Are Impractical

James Jordan and James Powell

James Jordan and James Powell are research professors at Poly-
technic University of New York. In this viewpoint, Jordan and
Powell argue that biofuels will not replace gasoline as a major
fuel source in the United States. According to the authors, the
energy derived from the yields of biofuel crops could at most
supply only 15 percent of U.S. fuel needs. Furthermore, they in-
sist the farmland devoted to biofuel crops would quickly become
depleted of nutrients needed to maintain soil fertility, leaving
fields difficult to reuse. Most important, wasting farmland in this
manner, Jordan and Powell assert, would deprive America of
food crops needed to feed the growing global population.

As you read, consider the following questions:

1. As the authors state, what is the fractional fuel
   value of ethanol in comparison to gasoline?

2. In the authors' view, how many gallons worth of ethanol would be produced by using all of America's farmland for ethanol production? What percentage of U.S. transport demands would be met by this production?

3. According to Jordan and Powell, why is Brazil a bad model for the potential U.S. conversion to ethanol fuel?

Biofuels such as ethanol made from corn, sugarcane, switchgrass and other crops are being touted as a "green" solution for a large part of America's transportation problem. Auto manufacturers, Midwest corn farmers and politicians are excited about ethanol. Initially, we, too, were excited about biofuels: no net carbon dioxide emissions, reduction of oil imports. Who wouldn't be enthusiastic?

But as we've looked at biofuels more closely, we've concluded that they're not a practical long-term solution to our need for transport fuels. Even if all of the 300 million acres (500,000 square miles) of currently harvested U.S cropland produced ethanol, it wouldn't supply all of the gasoline and diesel fuel we now burn for transport, and it would supply only about half of the needs for the year 2025. And the effects on land and agriculture would be devastating.

Ethanol's Poor Yield

It's difficult to understand how advocates of biofuels can believe they are a real solution to kicking our oil addiction. Agriculture Department studies of ethanol production from corn—the present U.S. process for ethanol fuel—find that an acre of corn yields about 139 bushels. At an average of about 2.5 gallons per bushel, the acre then will yield about 350 gallons of ethanol. But the fuel value of ethanol is only about two-thirds that of gasoline—1.5 gallons of ethanol in the tank equals 1 gallon of gasoline in terms of energy output.

Moreover, it takes a lot of input energy to produce ethanol: for fertilizer, harvesting, transport, corn processing, etc. After subtracting this input, the net positive energy available is less than half of the figure cited above. Some researchers even claim that the net energy of ethanol is actually negative when all inputs are included—it takes more energy to make ethanol than one gets out of it.

But allowing a net positive energy output of 30,000 British thermal units (Btu) per gallon, it would still take four gallons of ethanol from corn to equal one gallon of gasoline. The United States has 73 million acres of corn cropland. At 350 gallons per acre, the entire U.S. corn crop would make 25.5 billion gallons, equivalent to about 63 billion gallons of gasoline. The United States consumes 170 billion gallons of gasoline and diesel fuel annually. Thus the entire U.S. corn crop would supply only 3.7 percent of our auto and truck transport demands. Using the entire 300 million acres of U.S. cropland for corn-based ethanol production would meet about 15 percent of the demand.

Why Wastes Will Not Work

It is argued that rather than using corn to make ethanol, we can use agricultural wastes. But the amounts are still a drop in the bucket. Using the crop residues (called corn stover) from corn production could provide about 10 billion gallons per year of ethanol, according to a recent study by the U.S. Energy Information Administration. The net energy available would be greater than with ethanol from corn—about 60,000 Btu per gallon, equivalent to a half-gallon of gasoline. Still, all of the U.S. corn wastes would produce only the equivalent of 5 billion gallons of gasoline. Another factor to be considered: Not plowing wastes back into the land hurts soil fertility.

Similar limitations and problems apply to growing any crop for biofuels, whether switchgrass, hybrid willow, hybrid poplar or whatever. Optimistically, assuming that switchgrass

Survey Results Regarding What Fuel Should Replace Gasoline and Diesel in the United States

The fuel you would like to see replace petroleum is...	Share of Respondents		
	All respondents	Respondents who plan to purchase a small car	Respondents who plan to purchase an SUV
Biofuels*	24%	32%	21%
Electricity	16%	20%	10%
Hydrogen	14%	21%	11%
Other or no opinion	46%	27%	58%
All	100%	100%	100%

*Biofuels category includes: ethanol, corn, vegetable oil, alcohol, biodiesel, cooking oil, and soy beans.

TAKEN FROM: Opinion Research Corporation for National Renewable Energy Laboratory, September 22, 2005.

or some other crop could produce 1,000 gallons of ethanol per acre, over twice as much as we can get from corn plus stover, and that its net energy was 60,000 Btu per gallon, ethanol from 300 million acres of switchgrass still could not supply our present gasoline and diesel consumption, which is projected to double by 2025. The ethanol would meet less than half of our needs by that date.

Perhaps more important: The agricultural effects of such a large-scale program would be devastating.

Recently, there has been lots of excitement and media coverage about how Brazil produces ethanol for its automobile fuel and talk that America should follow its lead. But Brazil consumes only 10 billion gallons of gasoline and diesel fuel annually, compared with America's 170 billion. There are almost 4 million miles of paved roads in America—Brazil has 60,000. And Brazil is the leading producer of sugarcane—

more than 300 million tons annually—so it has lots of agricultural waste to make ethanol.

Cropland Should Be Reserved for Food Needs

Finally, considering projected population growth in the United States and the world, the humanitarian policy would be to maintain cropland for growing food—not fuel. Every day more than 16,000 children die from hunger-related causes—one child every five seconds. The situation will only get worse. It would be morally wrong to divert cropland needed for human food supply to powering automobiles. It would also deplete soil fertility and the long-term capability to maintain food production. We would destroy the farmland that our grandchildren and their grandchildren will need to live.

Periodical Bibliography

The following articles have been selected to supplement the diverse views presented in this chapter.

Adam Aston   "What Good Are Biofuels?" *Business Week*, November 13, 2006.

Jeffrey Ball   "Oil Companies Hope Grease Is the Word for Fuel," *Wall Street Journal*, June 25, 2007.

Jim Giles   "A Place in the Sun for Renewable Energy," *New Scientist*, May 5, 2007.

Charles Komanoff   "Whither Wind?" *Mother Earth News*, February/March 2007.

Clifford Krauss   "Green Gold, or Just Slime?" *New York Times*, March 7, 2007.

Steve Nash   "Decrypting Biofuel Scenarios," *Bioscience*, June 2007.

Alice Park   "Global Warming Survival Guide: What You Can Do: 1. Turn Food Into Fuel," *Time*, April 9, 2007.

Alexandra Shimo   "Thinking Big & Green," *Maclean's*, May 14, 2007.

Rebecca Smith   "The New Math of Alternative Energy," *Wall Street Journal*, February 12, 2007.

Will Thurmond   "Biodiesel's Bright Future," *Futurist*, July/August 2007.

Matt Vella   "Biofuel or Bust: On the Road with E85," *Wall Street Journal*, June 19, 2007.

Annette Von Jouanne   "Harvesting the Waves," *Mechanical Engineering*, December 2006.

Chris Wilson   "Harnessing a Mighty Force," *U.S. News & World Report*, June 4, 2007.

OPPOSING
VIEWPOINTS®
SERIES

CHAPTER 4

How Can the World's Resources Be Preserved?

Chapter Preface

According to various environmentalist organizations, the world's rainforests are disappearing at a rate of one and a half to two and a half acres every second. If the high estimate is accurate, it would mean that over 200,000 acres of rainforest are being lost every day. Though such figures are disputed, the rapid deforestation of these regions is a cause of concern to many and has inspired various organizations from grassroots collectives to the United Nations to take up the cause of rainforest conservation.

Rainforest regions are being cleared for two main reasons: to make way for croplands and livestock grazing ranges as well as to satisfy the native and foreign demands for cheap rainforest lumber. Because rainforest regions (especially in South America) are home to many impoverished communities, the opportunity to make a subsistence income through the cultivation of food crops, the raising of beef cattle, or the logging of desirable timber prompts native workers to consume the vast woodlands with little concern for conservation. The short-sighted destruction has been slowed in recent decades thanks to the cooperative efforts of indigenous farmers, national governments, and international ecology organizations.

In June 1995, the World Commission on Forests and Sustainable Development (WCFSD) met in Kalimantan (Indonesian Borneo) to discuss and promote policies that would get local communities involved in sustainable development of rainforest regions so that indigenous peoples could still harvest timber, medicines, nuts, spices, and other natural rainforest products while respecting regional biodiversity and replenishing areas for future use. Many who advocate saving the rainforests believe that getting local farmers, loggers, and governments involved in the process is the key to averting further destruction.

The WCFSD and other organizations also believe that education about the value of rainforest habitats and rainforest resources can make both local and global communities aware of the pressing need to save these regions. Many ecological alliances have spread the word to consumers and business in developed countries, for example, to avoid purchasing wood products that come from rainforest traders who do not practice sustainable development. In a 2003 *BusinessWeek* article, Mark L. Clifford and colleagues noted, "Ikea requires that all of its tropical hardwoods be cut in areas okayed by the Forest Stewardship Council, a German group that issues certificates to companies following sustainable practices." Some organizations have even staged boycotts of multinational conglomerates that continue to buy and sell rainforest resources that do not derive from protected, managed stocks.

Few environmentalists believe that the efforts made so far to foster a greater respect for the world's rainforests have stemmed the progress of destruction, but they attest that these tactics are a step in the right direction if that goal is to be reached. In chapter 4, analysts and commentators debate the ways in which other global resources can be preserved and shared. Though not all of the solutions offered compare to those directed at saving the rainforests, all possess a common understanding that the nations of the world must work in unison if global resources are to be conserved for future generations.

> *"[U]nless we collectively act to preserve the global environmental commons— the climate, the ozone layer, the diversity of life and the oceans—we will undermine the sustainability of national and regional development."*

A Commitment to Sustainable Development Will Help Preserve Global Resources

James D. Wolfensohn

James D. Wolfensohn is a former president of the World Bank, part of the World Bank Group, an international organization that provides capital and financial advice to countries for the purposes of economic development. In this viewpoint, Wolfensohn states that the World Bank is committed to the goal of reducing environmental degradation and the depletion of natural resources. He maintains that the bank and its partners (including the United Nations) have devised methods—such as the capping and trading of carbon emissions—to slow environmental harm. However, he asserts that all nations must utilize these mechanisms and show their commitment to environmental sustainability.

James D. Wolfensohn, "Global Priority," *Our Planet*, United Nations Environment Programme, 2002. Reproduced by permission.

As you read, consider the following questions:

1. What are the four global priorities that Wolfensohn suggests will help reverse environmental degradation in developing countries?

2. What two factors does Wolfensohn say limit many developing nations' abilities to think globally about preserving the environment?

3. What are the three market-oriented mechanisms that Wolfensohn mentions are being employed by the World Bank and its partners to help reduce carbon emissions?

The Millennium Development Goals (MDGs) [a set of goals to reduce poverty, disease, hunger, and other social ills by 2015] grew out of the agreements and resolutions of conferences organized by the United Nations in the past decade. They have now been commonly accepted as a framework for measuring development progress, and the World Bank Group is committed to working with our country partners to achieve these goals.

The MDGs can only be attained if countries choose an environmentally and socially sustainable development path. This requires managing the physical, human, natural and social capital that underpin development in ways that meet the needs of the present generation without foreclosing options for the future. This task is particularly challenging in the case of natural capital where the goods and services provided by ecological systems to sustain human development continue to be overexploited, degraded and—in cases such as biodiversity—irreversibly lost, on a scale that causes worldwide concern.

The Importance of Reducing Environmental Harm

There is broad agreement that reversing environmental degradation is critical to poverty reduction, since poor countries—

and particularly poor people—are most vulnerable to environmental degradation and lack the financial, technical and institutional means to address these problems. The priorities for action include:

- Improve access by poor people to safe water and sanitation and reduce indoor and outdoor air pollution to lessen the burden of disease.

- Arrest the degradation of soil and water resources to help improve agricultural productivity.

- Conserve terrestrial and aquatic ecosystems to preserve critical ecological goods and services.

- Improve social and economic conditions to help reduce the effects of environmental disasters.

Acting Collectively

Addressing these priorities—and building environmental sustainability at the country level—starts with sound national policies and programmes for economic growth that improve people's lives and the local environment. However, unless such national policies and programmes take into account adverse regional spill-over effects, they will potentially seriously threaten the health of transboundary ecosystems that provide vital environmental services to hundreds of millions of poor people. Moreover, unless we collectively act to preserve the global environmental commons—the climate, the ozone layer, the diversity of life and the oceans—we will undermine the sustainability of national and regional development. The evidence is unequivocal: regional and global environmental commons are, with few exceptions, deteriorating.

Environmental services constitute regional and global commons. They can be protected only through cooperation and collective action by developed and developing countries.

Helping our country partners address these challenges is the focus of the Bank's new environment strategy, Making

Sustainable Commitments. On many global environmental issues, Bank action is linked to the objectives of international agreements. The Bank Group works with country partners to overcome the factors that restrict their ability to act on global environmental priorities, particularly individual countries' limited economic incentives for taking action on the global environment, and the frequently weak national policy and institutional frameworks that limit the incentives and scope for effective action.

All Nations Must Think Globally

These limited economic incentives follow inherently from the regional or global public goods character of environmental services. As a consequence, decisions taken at the country level on the use of natural resources for national economic development do not adequately reflect their global impacts—or as the economists would say, the regional and global externalities are not internalized at the national level. Absent markets for trading certain global environmental goods and services, global non-market values are today captured primarily through international resource transfers. The Global Environment Facility (GEF) and the Multilateral Fund for the Implementation of the Montreal Protocol (MLF) were established to help underwrite and leverage such transfers.

Resource transfers from these mechanisms have served to raise the returns to host countries on environmentally friendly investments with global benefits, including energy services, rural development, management of terrestrial and aquatic ecosystems, and finding alternative technologies to replace chlorofluorocarbons and other ozone-threatening substances. Such investments can have a double benefit, contributing to long-term environmental sustainability—through, for example, reduced emissions of carbon dioxide—while also producing immediate local environmental benefits such as improved air quality.

The Environment Is Tied to the Lives of the World's Poor

The poor in the Global South are also the most vulnerable to environmental degradation. They depend on natural resources—soil, water, fisheries, forests—to provide their sustenance, and they suffer disproportionately from poor environmental conditions.

More than 65% of the world's poor are dependent on resource-based livelihoods, of which three-fourth are in food production and in fragile areas—steep hillsides, forest margins, and coastlines. In his Millennium Report, the Secretary General of the U.N. [Kofi Annan] highlighted the urgent need to secure the freedom of future generations to sustain their lives on this planet. He argued that "we have been blundering our children's heritage to pay for unsustainable practices."

Clearly, it makes little sense to lift people out of poverty today to have their children or grandchildren sink back into it tomorrow. A successful strategy for global poverty and human development must take in consideration the serious degradation of the environment and natural resources that underpin the lives and livelihoods of the world's poor and of future generations.

Mohamed T. El-Ashry,
"Human and Sustainable Development in the Global South,"
speech, American University Center for the Global South,
Washington, DC, April 8, 2003.

Partnership for Environmental Management

Together with the United Nations Development Programme and UNEP [United Nations Environment Programme], the World Bank Group has served as an implementing agency for the GEF and the MLF. We remain firmly committed to deliver on our mandates under these funding mechanisms, and strongly support expanded funding for the GEF to meet its broadening responsibilities. We see our role and impact going further: through these partnerships, we can help mobilize public funds for global environmental management, accelerate the transfer of environmentally friendly technologies to our developing country partners, and play a role—particularly through the Bank Group's International Finance Corporation—in promoting the global environment as a business opportunity.

The Bank Group's partnership with the GEF and the MLF has prompted a growing realization within our institution that global environmental needs have to be addressed as an extension of the local, national and regional environmental issues that underpin sustainable development. Through these alliances, we have embraced new financial mechanisms using limited grant resources, secured effective stakeholder involvement, and fostered partnerships of strategic importance for global environmental management.

Market Mechanisms to Reduce Carbon Emissions

A key challenge in our joint effort to promote public goods for the global environment is to help devise broader market-oriented mechanisms for dealing with long-term externalities, such as carbon emissions, where there is great scope for win-win solutions benefiting industrial and developing countries alike.

The development and management of the Prototype Carbon Fund (PCF) is a first step by the Bank Group in this direction. Participants in the $180 million PCF include 17 major corporations as well as six governments. The PCF seeks to demonstrate the feasibility of creating environmentally credible greenhouse gas emission reductions under the regulatory framework of the Kyoto Protocol's Clean Development Mechanism (CDM) and the development of a global market in which these would be traded.[1]

We are currently designing and marketing two new specialized funds: the Community Development Carbon Fund (CDCF) and the BioCarbon Fund (BioCF). The CDCF is designed to channel private capital under the CDM to small projects to the smallest and poorest countries. The BioCF is to develop prototypes for the production of environmentally and socially credible carbon assets through creation of carbon sinks in sustainable forestry, agriculture and management, and expanded biodiversity conservation efforts, consistent with the objectives of the Conventions on Biodiversity and Desertification.[2]

The Bank is committed, working in partnership with others, to support the priorities identified in the Plan of Action of the World Summit on Sustainable Development.

1. Under the Kyoto Protocol—an amendment to a UN treaty on climate control—nations are allotted greenhouse gas emission credits, which, if unused, can be traded to other countries that happen to exceed their allotted emissions. The United States has so far refused to ratify the agreement. It has already negotiated emission reductions purchase agreements in more than a dozen projects and countries.
2. The BioCarbon Fund was created to allow developing nations with few industrial carbon emissions to share in the benefits of carbon finance and trade. This is accomplished by funding and rewarding forestry and agribusiness projects that preserve areas where carbon gas is naturally utilized ("sinks"), such as forests and croplands. The Bank's efforts to create and sell certified improvements in biodiversity bundled with its carbon assets in its PCF business, and under the BioCF, signal the opportunity to create an independent market for biodiversity.

| *"Nobody can decide what is 'sustainable' for another person."*

Sustainable Development Privileges the Few Over the Many

Morgan J. Poliquin

In this viewpoint, Morgan J. Poliquin argues that sustainable development policies are unnecessary and intrusive. According to Poliquin, the principles of sustainable development are determined by large companies and international bodies that are interested in passing coercive policies to benefit their own profits or preserve their salaries. Poliquin contends that individuals, local businesses, and developing nations can best decide how to use resources according to their own needs; to allow corporations or external authorities to make these decisions is to submit to coercion. Morgan J. Poliquin is a geological engineer who manages an exploration company.

As you read, consider the following questions:

1. According to Poliquin, who coined the term "sustainable development"?

Morgan J. Poliquin, "'Sustainable Development' Privileges the Few," *Mises.org Daily Articles*, Ludwig Von Mises Institute, May 26, 2006. Reproduced by permission.

2. How does Poliquin utilize his mining analogy to comment on how scarce resources will be protected given simple market forces?

3. Who is hurt by sustainable development practices, according to the author?

Nomenclature and in particular, catchy phrases and slogans, are integral to the institution and leadership of political action and violence as well as simplifying or condensing the rationale for such action into neat and all encompassing phraseology.

Take for example, "from each according to ability, to each according to need." This trite phrase uttered by Bolsheviks [during the Russian Revolution] encapsulated the raison d'être and legitimized the terror inflicted by their foot soldiers against "bloodsuckers" and "enemies of the state" who were murdered and relieved of their property. Who was a bloodsucker or enemy of the state was decided upon by Bolshevik leadership.

In other words, the state, which manifests itself in the form of certain individuals supposedly acting on behalf of everyone, will determine what peoples' abilities and needs are. The problem with forcefully organizing society in this way is that every human is different, possessing unique abilities and needs according not to what someone in a position of power has allotted them, but to their own sensibilities.

Not only is [using] force to achieve these ends immoral, but it is impractical and wealth-destructive. We all condemn slavery, so why is it not immoral to force people to act in a way that is deemed to be beneficial to them?

Foisting Sustainable Development on the World

In 1987 a new but eerily similar political term was coined—"sustainable development"—which is defined as follows:

Development that meets the needs of the present without compromising the ability of future generations to meet their own needs.

This definition is attributed to Dr. Gro Harlem Brundtland, a medical doctor and the former Prime Minister of Norway, who, at the request of the then Secretary General of the United Nations, established and chaired the World Commission on Environment and Development. Her Committee produced a report entitled *Our Common Future* in which the definition first appeared.

Subsequent to the publication of the report, an enormous amount of meetings have been carried out, largely attended by state officials, state-financed intellectuals and the management of large corporations, to discuss the implications of such a statement and in particular its implementation in the form of coercive state regulations, which are coming into effect worldwide.

These regulations are far-reaching and designed to increasingly impact people's everyday decision making.

The private sector has been forced to swallow this new pill whole and almost without question. Companies are anxious to demonstrate how their practices are sustainable in order to curry favor with regulators.

This rush to compliance is all too reminiscent of the Y2K fiasco, when every company and organization was required, by law, to devote significant resources to demonstrating that they were *Y2K compliant*.

No Authority Can Determine Individual's Needs

Coercive communism is a failure because it consists of a self-appointed elite forcing needs and abilities upon people against their will. Needs and abilities cannot be determined arbitrarily by leaders; they stem from each person according to their own unique value system.

Sustainability Means Different Things to Different People

Because sustainability involves values, its meaning varies among individuals, groups, and societies, and changes over time. Prior to the nineteenth century the ideal landscape was agricultural. This was the landscape to be sustained, and in early America was considered the basis of Jeffersonian democracy. Today a landscape of small farmers is a quaint remembrance. Many urban residents of industrialized nations value wilderness, preferring recreation to commodity production. That value too may change. We should wonder why we fight political battles over sustaining forests that take centuries to mature, when centuries from now the debate may be moot.

Directing sustainability efforts in productive directions, then, requires understanding that it is a matter of values, not invariant biophysical processes. Some people and some ecosystems benefit from sustainability efforts, while others don't. When confronted with the term "sustainability," therefore, one should always ask: Sustain what, for whom, for how long, and at what cost?

Joseph A. Tainter, "A Framework for Sustainability,"
World Futures: The Journal of General Evolution,
vol. 59, nos. 3–4, April–June 2003, pp. 213–23.

Similarly, "enlightened" leaders should not be able to force us to act according to *their* assessment of what future generations' needs may be. Yet this is precisely what they propose.

Apart from the immorality of such an imposition, it doesn't even make sense practically. This is no more apparent than in one of the most integral of activities to industrial and modern society: mining. Anything we utilize has either been grown or mined. The most useful, sturdy and long lasting of things, such as concrete, steel and copper wire, are made from material that is mined.

Advantages of Renewing and Reusing

Metals are not naturally occurring in forms that are readily useful; formulae derived from experience and labor are required to produce metal in a useable form. The cost and effort to extract and refine elements such as iron and copper are so high that metal has always been recycled, which is possible because the properties of metals are not lessened by nature over time, unlike wood and other "farmed" substances.

The Bible speaks of turning swords into plowshares and that is what even industrial societies do today. For example, roughly 50% of all copper "consumed" in the United States is recycled. There are no government mandates that force this on people, it is just good sense on account of the fact that it is cheaper to melt a metal item and remake something new with it than to search for a new copper mine, develop it, dig out the copper, refine it and then make the new item.

In this very real sense, mining is infinitely sustainable; the needs of future generations will be met over and over again by the metal that past generations have found, extracted and refined. Before the metal was found, extracted, and mined, it was useless to humankind and there was nothing to even evaluate as sustainable. The fact that the metal has been removed from the ground and no longer exists there is not a sign of non-sustainability; rather it has created a permanent and unending supply of copper that can be recycled and reused ad infinitum.

Who Profits from Sustainable Development?

Legislating sustainability is another attempt to replace the collective decisions of many in the market place with the coercive will of the few. In a free market, with increasing scarcity of a given resource, its price tends to rise, encouraging economizing on behalf of those who consume the resource.

Why then all the fuss about making industries such as mining sustainable? Perhaps the people behind the legislation—the intellectuals, the legislators, and the large business firms that already dominate their industries—form an alliance that serves their own self-interests. The revered intellectuals sit on endless committees defining meaningless terms like *sustainable development* and are paid handsomely for doing so.

They are also lauded, much like actors, by their own organizations, which continually self-produce awards. Mingling with media, wealthy patrons, government officials, and business leaders, they frequent the most exclusive locations on the planet to discuss the implementation of their leadership. The self-interest of the legislators and government is readily apparent as their incomes are derived from the taxes that society is required to pay, purportedly for their management of the new laws and regulation that will ensure sustainable development.

Regulation Favors Large Firms

Established business firms would like to prevent others from offering similar services to those they provide. As Dr. Gabriel Kolko pointed out in his *Triumph of Conservatism*, the rise of government regulation in the 1900s in the United States resulted directly from the appeal for its implementation by established businesses.

Regulation, far from being established by altruistic intellectuals and far-sighted politicians, creates government-enforced cartels for (and was conceived by) the established businesses that were losing their command of the marketplace to new business that were providing cheaper and better products and services.

The regulation favored the large, established firms. The implementation of sustainable practices is condoned, supported, lauded, and financed by the big businesses of today.

Like their 19th-century counterparts, they have the accounting staff and present infrastructure to handle the extra costs of becoming "sustainable." It is the little guy—the new entrepreneur—who is paralyzed by the burden of the new legislation.

The enlightened intellectuals behind sustainability today are likely dupes who are happy to exchange accolades, notoriety, and large UN salaries for creating nonsensical legislation that only serves to inhibit new enterprise and entrench established business interests.

Everyone Else Loses

Who is hurt by this? Certainly anybody who would like to enter a new business into the marketplace, but more importantly it is the consumers of the products these industries produce who are harmed. Coercive legislation reduces the diversity of quality and prices among competing products. It robs consumers of options, raises prices, and destroys wealth.

Nobody can decide what is "sustainable" for another person. Every action requires a weighing up of costs and benefits. To implement any one person's idea of sustainability on everyone else will result in loss. The idea that people are not able to make these decisions on their own, and require leadership and coercive laws to determine what is best for them, is essentially to implement slavery.

Communists told us to follow them because humanity was at stake. Today we are told that the planet itself is at stake. It sounds like a new way of saying the same old thing. To sacrifice the needs of individuals for the sake of the many will result in great benefits to the very few, at the cost of the many.

"*Sharing essential resources will quite simply allow some 50,000 people to live who would otherwise continue to die needlessly every day.*"

Nations Must Share Equally the World's Resources

Rajesh Makwana

In this viewpoint, Rajesh Makwana states that a large percentage of the world's population is denied access to global resources. To avoid this predicament, Makwana proposes that the international community share all common resources such as food, water, oil, and medicine. In Makwana's view, sharing will undo competition for these resources and relax international tensions while bettering the lives of those who are trapped by poverty and hunger in developing nations. To adopt this new economic principle, however, Makwana contends that developed nations that currently consume more than their share of resources will have to learn to live with less and sacrifice for the global good. Rajesh Makwana is the director of Share the World's Resources, an organization that promotes global justice.

Rajesh Makwana, "Sharing: A Natural Law of Economy," *Share the World's Resources* (www.stwr.net), June 7, 2007. Reproduced by permission.

As you read, consider the following questions:

1. According to Makwana, what are the two assumptions that the world community must make in order to adopt sharing resources as the guiding economic principle?
2. Who have been the main beneficiaries of over-consumption, in Makwana's view?
3. As Makwana predicts, how will sharing resources impact international relations?

Whilst the world economy continues to globalise market forces, the basic needs of the majority [of the] world are still not being met, and an estimated 50,000 people [are] dying each day, having been denied access to essential resources.

In 1948, the General Assembly of the United Nations adopted the Universal Declaration of Human Rights. All member states absolutely agreed that the universal provision of adequate food, water, housing, health care, education, political participation and employment must be the priority of all governments. After 59 years we may well have landed on the moon, created cyber-technology and witnessed an information revolution, but around half the world still doesn't have access to essential resources such as clean water, adequate food and basic medicines.

Clearly a fundamental shift in national and international social and economic policy is long overdue. Ensuring that people are not living in perpetual poverty or dying needlessly constitutes a moral and economic necessity for all nations.

Transforming the Global Economy

Addressing these issues at a fundamental level requires a restructuring of the global economy and a reframing of our values and priorities. By replacing the competitive self-interest of market forces with cooperation and sharing as our primary distributive process, the 'operating system' upon which the international economy is organised can lead to a sustainable world based on social and economic justice. This in turn can create more peaceful international relations.

Sharing those resources which are essential to life—currently denied to 40 percent of the world population—can rapidly reduce poverty and inequality. Sharing can also address the key economic issues of our time such as the excessive power of corporations and market forces, outdated neoliberal policy, a defunct IMF [International Monetary Fund]/World Bank, a biased free-trade regime, and stagnant international aid efforts. Sharing, in essence, favours the whole and not the part.

Preconditions to Sharing

Sharing is a simple word, yet sharing essential resources will require a significant overhaul of the global economy, which inevitably presents a daunting challenge.

There are some crucial assumptions that must be accepted if the international community is to consider sharing as a serious alternative to competition over key resources without being dissuaded by the sheer scale of the task ahead:

- The single most important task for all governments must be to eradicate poverty, create greater equality, ensure environmental sustainability and guarantee that basic human rights and needs are secured—FOR ALL PEOPLE.

- The present international political and economic architecture is unsustainable and unable to secure basic human rights. It must be restructured according to more humane values.

It is only from this position that we can move forward and propose how to create a better world.

When considering sharing as a mechanism for organising the global economy, it is important to emphasise the universal and human qualities of the principle of sharing.

Unlike socialism, capitalism or communism, sharing is not an ideology or an 'ism', and certainly not a concept which can give rise to a rigid set of beliefs and doctrines.

What is Sharing?

Sharing simply means 'having in common' or 'using something jointly with others', a natural human behaviour that is applied daily in the lives of most people. We all accept the need to share space, responsibilities and food on a family and community basis, but neglect to recognise that the same basic principle of sharing must be followed on an international basis.

Examples of sharing on a national and international scale include:

The Marshall Plan. After World War II, US Secretary of State George C. Marshall initiated a mammoth four-year program of aid for a devastated Europe experiencing extreme poverty, hunger and economic stagnation. The results were unprecedented. Europe quickly recovered and the positive political and economic ramifications for both the US and Europe are still observable. The Marshall Plan was an important example of how sharing resources, in this case financial resources, could benefit all parties.

Venezuela. Sharing can also be seen as an economic process in Latin America. Venezuela shares its oil with a number of other countries in the region, such as Bolivia and Cuba. Countries like Cuba, in return, provide the majority of doctors that work in Venezuela. As a consequence of sharing in this way, political relationships and goodwill between the nations involved are reinforced.

But sharing is not necessarily undertaken as a form of exchange. Venezuela also shares its oil farther afield with the poor in the US, Cuba, which boasts an excellent domestic healthcare system, is well known for sending medical staff all over the developing world. In fact, they have a medical army of greater numbers than the World Health Organization.

The Welfare State. National welfare systems can also be interpreted as systems of sharing. Society pools its resources, through taxation, to ensure that education, health care, housing and unemployment benefits are available to all. In this way, society creates a social safety net to ensure that the basic rights and needs of the population are met.

The impetus for sharing must be altruistic, but this is not to say that there will be no mutual benefit involved. Sharing occurs as a result of an acceptance of unity or solidarity—whether between people or between nations. Importantly, sharing also has the potential of creating that same sense of unity and solidarity, and in this way becoming a self-reinforcing process.

Sadly, when we look at a nation's relationship with the wider international community, the principle of sharing is disregarded. Given the increasingly interdependent nature of the world and the globalised systems of commerce and finance, the welfare of numerous low-income countries depends directly on economically dominant nations and their policies for trade and development. Despite the globalization of free-market policies, wealthy nations neglect to create a global safety net to protect poor people in low-income countries from dying of hunger, let alone provide any unemployment benefits. . . .

Sharing as an Organising Principle in the Global Economy

The process of privatisation is at the heart of the market system. The privatisation and enclosure of common resources since the Middle Ages has steadily increased in tandem with

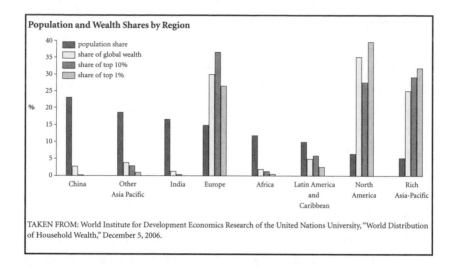

Population and Wealth Shares by Region

- population share
- share of global wealth
- share of top 10%
- share of top 1%

TAKEN FROM: World Institute for Development Economics Research of the United Nations University, "World Distribution of Household Wealth," December 5, 2006.

commercialisation, reaching its zenith with the enforcement of corporate intellectual property rights over forms of life such as plant species.

Apart from our global ecological system, shared resources include all creations of nature, including land (and those resources land contains), water and sources of energy. The concept of the global commons can be extended to include the creations of society, particularly if these creations can be deemed necessary to meet basic human requirements—such as information about disease eradication and heath care, and technologies, such as water purification devices or communication equipment. These resources should not be permitted to be monopolized exclusively by private interests with a view only to profiteering.

Most importantly, if the world is to cooperate to ensure basic human needs are provided, it is imperative that common resources are cooperatively owned by the global public and do not fall under national interests. Without this affirmation of international unity, confrontation between nations over resources will continue. Given the uneven distribution of certain resources around the world, without an international shared ownership agreement it would be difficult to ensure basic needs are secured globally.

Rich Countries Must Learn to Live Simply

In order to share the world's resources, rich countries must make the sacrifice of learning how to live a simpler, more sustainable lifestyle, so that 'others may simply live'. The economic and frugal use of those resources which are essential to life is a preliminary condition that a donor country, wishing to share its resources with the international community, must abide by. Many environmental organisations and NGOs [nongovernmental organizations] like the Centre for the Advancement of the Steady State Economy (CASSE) have been advocating a similar position for many years.

Even though there is enough food produced in the world to provide 4.3 pounds of food for every man, woman and child every day, it is disproportionately distributed—or simply wasted—by the developed world. Sharing efficiently will necessitate a redistribution of existing resources. Countries with a greater endowment of a resource must redistribute a portion of their endowment to a country where that same resource in under-supplied.

Over-consumption in general, although common in wealthy countries, does little to increase the well-being of the population whilst seriously damaging the environment through the resultant CO_2 emissions. Corporations have been the main beneficiaries of over-production and over-consumption, yet even their security is now threatened by the potential environmental, social, political and financial impacts which are the natural outcomes of one-sided excess. These factors are expected to eventually catalyse public demand for change, even in wealthy countries.

Over-consuming countries like the United States must take the lead in creating the necessary change in the political, economic and social fabric of the world. They must actively redistribute the fruits of their production and contribute their expertise and labour to ensure that resources can be shared effectively. Government intervention under international mandates will be necessary to facilitate this process.

Organising Global Redistribution and Sharing Networks

It is the international community that collectively should determine which resources are essential for meeting basic human needs and must therefore be shared globally. Once decided, the sharing or redistribution of these resources will need to be coordinated in a logical and democratic manner.

At present, the United Nations, although flawed and impotent, is the only body which could serve as the coordinators of a global system of sharing. With an international membership and humanitarian charter, the UN system is clearly the only international agency with the experience and resources to address global economic reform.

It will be necessary to create an additional body within the UN responsible for coordinating the pooling and sharing of global resources to meet the basic needs of the global public. For the time being we may call such a body the 'UN Council for Resource Sharing (UNCRS)'.

The UNCRS would set up and coordinate a Global Sharing Network (GSN), a system that acts upon information from governments around the world. The GSN would measure the changing levels of excess production in each country and then calculate how much of any resource a country is able to redistribute to another. . . .

How Sharing Can Benefit the Developing World

Sharing essential resources will quite simply allow some 50,000 people to live who would otherwise continue to die needlessly every day. Through the Global Sharing Network and the coordinated activity of NGOs and civil society groups, whole villages could receive enough food, water and medicine to ensure their survival.

Providing the necessary infrastructure, expertise, labour and technology will also be part of this process, and would be shared by donor countries. The necessary resources for hospitals, educational facilities and housing would also follow. The majority of these resources would be transferred from where they are in excess in the global north to where they are most urgently required in the global south.

The process of sharing basic resources in this way is a direct route to economic development. This system can ensure a 'bottom up' development controlled by those most affected, and not an imposed 'top-down' process. Financial aid would no longer be provided to corrupt governments who could squander it or use it to repay debt. Strengthening local communities in this way will empower and enable them to become self-sufficient, which is likely to have significant impacts on social and political cohesion.

How Sharing Can Affect the Global Economy

Implementing a system of sharing would have significant impact on international trade, finance and development, and thereby directly affect the activities of the WTO [World Trade Organization], IMF and World Bank [i.e., international bodies that oversee and finance economic development].

Adopting a system of sharing will mean that the majority of commodities and goods that are currently traded would instead be cooperatively owned and distributed by the global public through the UNCRS. Such resources include energy supplies and the provision of utilities such as water, essential agricultural produce required for food, cotton for clothing, essential healthcare services, equipment and medication, essential knowledge and technology and resources for providing education. As a result, international trade in commodities and their derivatives will be significantly reduced and confined to non-essential goods.

Sharing will ensure that essential domestic needs are largely met at the local level, reducing dependency on foreign imports of essential goods. As a consequence, there would be less need for developing countries to agree to prohibitive trade agreements, whether multilateral or bilateral. This would free the population to develop their own industry and economy. . . .

What Will Sharing Mean for International Relations

There is no doubt that replacing the competitive self-interest that exists between nations and upon which the global economy is based, with a cooperative system of sharing resources, will lead to more harmonious international relations.

People in developing countries will be directly aided by the 'richer' nations in their regions and across the world, a process that will likely create much goodwill and tolerance between and within each country. In this sense, sharing resources presents a better foreign policy tool than the forceful acquisition and conflicts over resources that are the hallmarks of the modern world.

As marginalisation decreases in the developing world, the urge to terrorise and fight against the dominant powers will most likely subside to a large extent.

It is also possible that the new altruistic ethos that sharing can encourage, particularly in 'donor' countries, will have a beneficial effect on social consciousness and fill the void in community relations and purpose that has grown alongside commercialisation.

The mutual benefit of sharing will be best realised once the developing world is living healthily and in a self sustaining manner. At this stage, international trade and exchange is likely to increase significantly as development proceeds and societies share their cultural inheritance.

Sharing in the way described is essentially a democratic and participatory process. Once economic and social justice has been achieved, these democratic structures can be utilised to further a nation's integration into a democratic global community. A representative global governance structure may be a much needed side-effect of this process.

A Campaign for Global Economic Reform

The role of any campaign for sharing the world's resources is not to dictate the terms of reform but to direct attention to what needs reforming and to propose alternatives.

Sharing provides that alternative, allowing resource allocation to occur cooperatively under the democratic guidance of the global public and entirely for their benefit. Sharing creates efficiency, not through the market mechanism, but through the reduction of over-consumption and resource depletion.

Sharing also lessens competition and promotes cooperation between nations. Most importantly, sharing can rapidly relieve poverty and reduce inequality.

Economists have long known about the antagonism between the market and the environment yet stick to the 'market mantra' for lack of an alternative. If the global community is serious about creating a sustainable economy and ending poverty, a system of sharing essential resources is an intensely practical and humane alternative.

> *"So-called 'free trade agreements' threaten to erode many of the advances in global environmental protection, endangering our planet and the natural resources necessary to support life."*

Free-Trade Agreements Need to Be Repealed to Preserve Global Resources

Deborah James

In this viewpoint, Deborah James opposes international free trade agreements on the grounds that they fail to protect global resources and they damage the environment. James contends that free trade agreements typically provide multinational corporations with the power to dictate how national resources can be used, leaving many developing nations open to exploitation. Such exploitation has little regard for protected environments, James asserts, and threatens the biodiversity as well as the cultural diversity of entire regions. Deborah James is the director of the World Trade Organization Program at Global Trade Watch, a progressive organization that promotes fair trade.

Deborah James, "Free Trade and the Environment," *Global Exchange*, 2005. Reproduced by permission.

As you read, consider the following questions:

1. According to James, in what ways do free trade agreements "prohibit member countries from enacting many new environmental regulations?"
2. What is "bioprospecting," as James describes it?
3. What is Chapter 11 of the North American Free Trade Agreement, and why does James believe it is a detrimental part of such free trade agreements?

For decades, governments have worked together through the United Nations to develop agreements to protect the natural resources of our shared planet. Unfortunately, so-called "free trade agreements" threaten to erode many of the advances in global environmental protection, endangering our planet and the natural resources necessary to support life. The North American Free Trade Agreement (NAFTA) and certain agreements of the World Trade Organization (WTO) were written to prioritize rights for corporations over protections for our shared environment.

But rather than being repealed, corporate interests are negotiating the expansion of these corporate rights. The U.S.-Dominican Republic-Central American Free Trade Agreement (CAFTA) . . . and the proposed Free Trade Area of the Americas (FTAA), currently in negotiations, are modeled on NAFTA. In addition, negotiations are proceeding within the WTO to expand many of its policies.

These new agreements threaten global biodiversity, would accelerate the spread of genetically engineered (GE) crops, increase natural resource exploitation, further degrade some of the most critical environmental regions on the planet, and erode the public's ability to protect our planet for future generations.

No Protections for the Environment

Neither CAFTA nor the FTAA require member countries to adopt internationally recognized standards for environmental protection. Nor does either agreement ensure that member countries don't lower or waive their existing environmental laws in an effort to attract investment. What's more, rules in CAFTA and the FTAA would actually prohibit member countries from enacting many new environmental regulations, allowing those regulations to be challenged as "barriers to trade." This strips the public from a fundamental democratic right to pass laws that protect our environment in favor of corporations' "right" to profit from environmental destruction.

Mega-Diverse Countries Imperiled

Latin America is one of the most biologically and culturally diverse regions on the planet. Four of the five Central American countries included in CAFTA have tropical areas that have been identified as "critical regions" for their biodiversity. Additionally, 7 of the world's 12 "megadiverse" countries, (Mexico, Brazil, Venezuela, Peru, Ecuador, Costa Rica and Colombia) are found in the Americas. "Mega-diversity" countries represent the majority of the world's biodiversity and surviving Indigenous peoples, the true guardians of biodiversity. Unfortunately, so-called "free trade" agreements directly contradict important international legislation designed to protect the rights of Indigenous peoples and biodiversity, like the Convention on Biological Diversity as well as the International Labor Organization Convention 169, which states that Indigenous groups must be consulted on issues that affect their rights to land and livelihood.

Piracy of Global Biodiversity

In the last decade, the biodiversity of the Americas has been targeted by "life science" corporations (the growing consolidation of pharmaceutical, agrichemical and seed companies) in search of "green gold." These corporations are pillaging humankind's patrimony of traditional knowledge and biodiversity to create and patent drugs and agricultural products to sell for profit. The quest to patent life forms, especially medicinal plants and crops, threatens our food security, access to healthcare, and the biological and cultural diversity of the Americas.

Intellectual property rules in CAFTA and the FTAA would require that member countries grant protections to the patenting of life forms. This would facilitate a massive increase in "bioprospecting" or the practice of corporations patenting Indigenous communities' knowledge of plants and then profiting from that knowledge—while forcing Indigenous communities to pay for what they had previously held in common.

No GE Food Labeling and Crop Contamination

Despite the fact that independent polls in virtually every country on the planet demonstrate that people want genetically engineered (GE) foods labeled, corporations and the U.S. government have refused to do so. Giant agribusiness multinationals ADM and Cargill have generally refused to segregate GE from non-GE crops, eliminating consumer choice and imposing GE foods on consumers. With CAFTA and the FTAA, labeling laws would be prohibited as "more burdensome than necessary" for agribusiness investors.

Dozens of crops have been developed and domesticated in the Americas over the last 10,000 years, including corn and potatoes, two of the world's most important crops for food security. The traditional cradles of food diversity are threatened by encroaching genetic contamination. The experience of Mexico under NAFTA offers an example of what's to come for Central America under CAFTA. NAFTA forced open protected Mexican corn markets to a flood of cheap imports of corn from the U.S. Corn imports into Mexico have displaced at least one and a half million farmers and are steadily eroding the genetic diversity of thousands of native corn varieties.

Free Trade Agreement, cartoon. Copyright © 2003 by Arcadio Esquivel and Cagle-cartoons.com. All rights reserved.

Then, in September 2001, genetic contamination of native corn varieties was discovered as a result of the introduction of artificially low-priced GE corn from the United States under NAFTA. The expansion of GE crops threatens food security around the world.

CAFTA and the FTAA completely disregard international law, such as the Cartagena Protocol on Biosafety, designed to regulate the cultivation and trade of genetically modified organisms.

Expanding the Rights of Big Business

While limiting public regulation for environmental protections, CAFTA and the FTAA would grant expansive powers to corporations. CAFTA's investor protections are modeled after one of the most hotly contested sections in NAFTA—its Chapter 11—a virtual Bill of Rights for corporations. These provisions allow corporations to sue governments for "damages" if a government law affects their profits. Chapter 11 of NAFTA has undermined the sovereignty of democratically elected governments, and their ability to act in the public interest. An issue over a Quebec environmental law banning specific pesticides reveals how these provisions undermine environmental protection.

Quebec law bans a popular weed killer called 2,4-D, which is considered a possible human carcinogen, and has been shown to adversely affect the immune system and reproductive functions in humans, among other impacts.

But now a corporate lobbying group representing some of the makers of the pesticide are threatening to challenge the law by suing the Canadian government under NAFTA's Chapter 11. The provincial government of Quebec and Canadian taxpayers have been given a harsh choice: pay the corporations millions of dollars in future lost profits, or repeal the law. Similar Chapter 11 cases have led to the overturn of environmental laws and millions of dollars in fines paid to corporations. If CAFTA is enacted, investor-to-state lawsuits will be spread to the corporations of six additional countries, threatening critical environmental protection in the U.S. and Central America.

Limiting Public Regulations

Both CAFTA and an agreement currently under negotiation in the WTO covering Services would make it increasingly difficult for governments to regulate and limit multinational corporate activity in environmentally damaging activities such as oil extraction, forestry, electricity generation, road construction, and waste incineration in the interests of environmental protection.

In addition, under the proposed WTO rules on Services, governments could be required to let foreign corporations violate environmental standards. For instance, requirements that that a percentage of electricity be produced from environmentally friendly energy sources could be found to "discriminate" against foreign service companies if those companies don't provide environmentally friendly energy, and would have to be scrapped under proposed WTO rules—even if the standard is the most effective way to protect the environment.

Dropping Protective Tariffs

Corporate interests are also negotiating the expansion of the WTO through an agreement on Non-Agricultural Market Access, or NAMA. Primarily involving industrial manufactured goods, NAMA also includes trade in natural resources such as forest products, gems and minerals, and fishing and fish products. NAMA aims to reduce tariffs as well as decreasing or eliminating so-called Non-Tariff Barriers (NTBs), which can include measures for environmental protection and community development.

Eliminating tariffs in natural resources would dramatically increase their exploitation. The World Forum of Fish-harvesters and Fish-workers has warned of the devastation to fish conservation posed by NAMA. Even the U.S. Trade Representative has acknowledged that eliminating tariffs on wood products would dramatically increase logging, exacerbating deforestation in some of the world's most sensitive forests.

The WTO has already identified a wide range of environmental policy tools as potential 'barriers to trade': the certification of sustainably harvested wood and fish products; restrictions on trade in harmful chemicals; and packaging, marketing, and labeling requirements such as organic and Fair Trade labeling.

Increased Trade Increases Dependency on Oil

Increasing trade increases our consumption of and dependency on oil, which has created a massive global crisis of human-induced climate change. The rise of global temperatures means more severe droughts and floods that will literally change the face of the Earth; the loss of coastal lands and the destruction of forests; an increase in heat waves and other human health hazards; and the extinction of plant and animal species. Our consumption of oil also leads to violations of the human rights of peoples in oil-producing countries such as Ecuador, Colombia, Indonesia, and Nigeria, who suffer environmental heath problems, displacement, and contamination of their communities. Increased trade—and hence dependence on oil—will also contribute to global insecurity by providing further incentive for the drive towards war as the U.S. government struggles for control over this most strategic global resource.

"Water must be declared and understood for all time to be the common property of all."

Water Must Be Made a Public Resource

Maude Barlow and Tony Clarke

Maude Barlow is the chairperson of the Council of Canadians, a liberal organization that champions fair trade, water rights, and health care. Tony Clarke is the director of the Polaris Institute, a Canadian think tank dedicated to democratic social change. Barlow and Clarke are also the authors of Blue Gold: The Fight to Stop the Corporate Theft of the World's Water. *In this viewpoint, Barlow and Clarke argue that globalization and international free trade agreements are putting the world's water supplies in the hands of big corporations. Instead of managing these resources for the good of local and global populations, the authors claim that these corporations are using their leverage over water supplies to make money. Barlow and Clarke insist that water must be decommodified and made a public resource with international protections so that it cannot be depleted or degraded by profit-driven entities.*

As you read, consider the following questions:

1. According to the authors, how are Third World countries being forced to contract with foreign water cartels instead of relying on local water resources?

2. How are free-trade agreements affecting water rights, in the view of Barlow and Clarke?

3. On what two principles will the management of water be based if privatization of global water resources occurs? On what principle do Barlow and Clarke contend that water management should be based?

Humanity is polluting, diverting and depleting the well-spring of life at a startling rate. With every passing day, our demand for fresh water outpaces its availability, and thousands more people are put at risk. Already, the social, political and economic impacts of water scarcity are rapidly becoming a destabilizing force, with water-related conflicts springing up around the globe. Quite simply, unless we dramatically change our ways, between one-half and two-thirds of humanity will be living with severe freshwater shortages within the next quarter-century.

It seemed to sneak up on us, or at least those of us living in the North. Until the past decade, the study of fresh water was left to highly specialized groups of experts—hydrologists, engineers, scientists, city planners, weather forecasters and others with a niche interest in what so many of us took for granted. Many knew about the condition of water in the Third World, including the millions who die of waterborne diseases eyed year. But this was seen as an issue of poverty, poor sanitation and injustice—all areas that could be addressed in the just world for which we were fighting.

Now, however, an increasing number of voices—including human rights and environmental groups, think tanks and research organizations, official international agencies and thousands of community groups around the world—are sounding the alarm. The earth's fresh water is finite and small, representing less than one half of 1 percent of the world's total water stock. Not only are we adding 85 million new people to the planet every year, but our per capita use of water is doubling every twenty years, at more than twice the rate of human population growth. A legacy of factory farming, flood irrigation, the construction of massive dams, toxic dumping, wetlands and forest destruction, and urban and industrial pollution has damaged the Earth's surface water so badly that we are now mining the underground water reserves far faster than nature can replenish them.

The earth's "hot sirens"—areas where water reserves are disappearing—include the Middle East, Northern China, Mexico, California and almost two dozen countries in Africa. Today thirty-one countries and over 1 billion people completely lack access to clean water. Every eight seconds a child dies from drinking contaminated water. The global freshwater crisis looms as one of the greatest threats ever to the survival of our planet.

The Drive to Privatize

Tragically, this global call for action comes in an era guided by the principles of the so-called Washington Consensus, a model of economics rooted in the belief that liberal market economics constitutes the one and only economic choice for the whole world. Competitive nation-states are abandoning natural resources protection and privatizing their ecological commons. Everything is now for sale, even those areas of life, such as social services and natural resources, that were once considered the common heritage of humanity. Governments around the world are abdicating their responsibilities to protect the natural resources in their territory, giving authority away to the private companies involved in resource exploitation.

Faced with the suddenly well-documented freshwater crisis, governments and international institutions are advocating a Washington Consensus solution: the privatization and commodification of water. Price water, they say in chorus: put it up for sale and let the market determine its future. For them, the debate is closed. Water, say the World Bank and the United Nations, is a "human need," not a "human right." These are not semantics: the difference in interpretation is crucial. A human need can be supplied many ways, especially for those with money. No one can sell a human right.

So a handful of transnational corporations, backed by the World Bank and the International Monetary Fund, are aggressively taking over the management of public water services in countries around the world, dramatically raising the price of water to the local residents and profiting especially from the Third World's desperate search for solutions to its water crisis. Some are startlingly open: the decline in freshwater supplies and standards has created a wonderful venture opportunity for water corporations and their investors, they boast. The agenda is clear: Water should be treated like any other tradable good, with its use determined by the principles of profit.

It should come as no surprise that the private sector knew before most of the world about the looming water crisis and has set out to take advantage of what it considers to be blue gold. According to *Fortune*, the annual profits of the water industry now amount to about 40 percent of those of the oil sector and are already substantially higher than the pharmaceutical sector, now close to $1 trillion. But only about 5 percent of the world's water is currently in private hands, so it is clear that we are talking about huge profit potential as the water crisis worsens. In 1999 there were more than $15 billion worth of water acquisitions in the US water industry alone, and all the big water companies are now listed on the stock exchanges.

The Water Lords

There are ten major corporate players now delivering freshwater services for profit. The two biggest are both from France— Vivendi Universal and Suez—considered to be the General Motors and Ford of the global water industry. Between them, they deliver private water and wastewater services to more than 200 million customers in 150 countries and are in a race, along with others such as Bouygues Saur, RWE—Thames Water and Bechtel United Utilities, to expand to every corner of the globe. In the United States, Vivendi operates through its subsidiary, USFilter; Suez via its subsidiary, United Water; and RWE by way of American Water Works.

They are aided by the World Bank and the IMF, which are increasingly forcing Third World countries to abandon their public water delivery systems and contract with the water giants in order to be eligible for debt relief. The performance of these companies in Europe and the developing world has been well documented: huge profits, higher prices for water, cutoffs to customers who cannot pay, no transparency in their dealings, reduced water quality, bribery and corruption.

Water for profit takes a number of other forms. The bottled-water industry is one of the fastest-growing and least regulated industries in the world, expanding at an annual rate of 20 percent. Last year close to 90 billion liters of bottled water were sold around the world—most of it in nonreusable plastic containers, bringing in profits of $22 billion to this highly polluting industry. Bottled-water companies like Nestlé, Coca-Cola and Pepsi are engaged in a constant search for new water supplies to feed the insatiable appetite of this business. In rural communities all over the world, corporate interests are buying up farmlands, indigenous lands, wilderness tracts and whole water systems, then moving on when sources are depleted. Fierce disputes are being waged in many places over these "water takings," especially in the Third World. As one company explains, water is now "a rationed necessity that may be taken by force."

Corporations are now involved in the construction of massive pipelines to carry fresh water long distances for commercial sale while others are constructing supertankers and giant sealed water bags to transport vast amounts of water across the ocean to paying customers. Says the World Bank, "One way or another, water will soon be moved around the world as oil is now." The mass movement of bulk water could have catalytic environmental impacts. Some proposed projects would reverse the flow of mighty rivers in Canada's north, the environmental impact of which would be greater than China's Three Gorges Dam.

Signing Away Water Rights Through Free Trade Agreements

At the same time, governments are signing away their control over domestic water supplies to trade agreements such as the North American Free Trade Agreement, its expected successor, the Free Trade Area of the Americas (FTAA), and the World Trade Organization. These global trade institutions effectively give transnational corporations unprecedented access to the freshwater resources of signatory countries. Already, corporations have started to sue governments in order to gain access to domestic water sources and, armed with the protection of these international trade agreements, are setting their sights on the commercialization of water.

Water is listed as a "good" in the WTO and NAFTA, and as an "investment" in NAFTA. It is to be included as a "service" in the upcoming WTO services negotiations (the General Agreement on Trade in Services [GATS]) and in the FTAA. Under the "National Treatment" provisions of NAFTA and the GATS, signatory governments who privatize municipal water services will be obliged to permit competitive bids from tran-

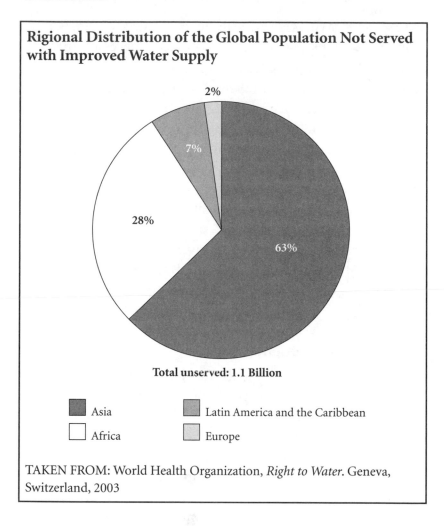

Rigional Distribution of the Global Population Not Served with Improved Water Supply

2%

7%

28%

63%

Total unserved: 1.1 Billion

- Asia
- Africa
- Latin America and the Caribbean
- Europe

TAKEN FROM: World Health Organization, *Right to Water*. Geneva, Switzerland, 2003

snational water-service corporations. Similarly, once a permit is granted to a domestic company to export water for commercial purposes, foreign corporations will have the right to set up operations in the host country.

NAFTA contains a provision that requires "proportional sharing" of energy resources now being traded between the signatory countries. This means that the oil and gas resources no longer belong to the country of extraction, but are a shared resource of the continent. For example, under NAFTA, Canada now exports 57 percent of its natural gas to the United States and is not allowed to cut back on these supplies, even to cut fossil fuel production under the Kyoto accord. Under this same provision, if Canada started selling its water to the United States—which President [George W.] Bush has already said he considers to be part of the United States' continental energy program—the State Department would consider it to be a trade violation if Canada tried to turn off the tap. And under NAFTA's "investor state" Chapter 11 provision, American corporate investors would be allowed to sue Canada for financial losses. Already, [a] California company is suing the Canadian government for $10.5 billion because the province of British Columbia banned the commercial export of bulk water.

The WTO also opens the door to the commercial export of water by prohibiting the use of export controls for any "good" for any purpose. This means that quotas or bans on the export of water imposed for environmental reasons could be challenged as a form of protectionism. At the December 2001 Qatar ministerial meeting of the WTO, a provision was added to the so-called Doha Text, which requires governments to give up "tariff" and "non-tariff" barriers—such as environmental regulations—to environmental services, which include water.

The Case Against Privatization

If all this sounds formidable, it is. But the situation is not without hope. For the fact is, we know how to save the world's water: reclamation of despoiled water systems, drip irrigation over flood irrigation, infrastructure repairs, water conservation, radical changes in production methods and watershed management, just to name a few. Wealthy industrialized countries could supply every person on earth with clean water if they canceled the Third World debt, increased foreign aid payments and placed a tax on financial speculation.

None of this will happen, however, until humanity earmarks water as a global commons and brings the rule of law—local, national and international—to any corporation or government that dares to contaminate it. If we allow the commodification of the world's freshwater supplies, we will lose the capacity to avert the looming water crisis. We will be allowing the emergence of a water elite that will determine the world's water future in its own interest. In such a scenario, water will go to those who can afford it and not to those who need it.

This is not an argument to excuse the poor way in which some governments have treated their water heritage, either squandering it, polluting it or using it for political gain. But the answer to poor nation-state governance is not a nonaccountable transnational corporation but good governance. For governments in poor countries, the rich world's support should go not to profiting from bad water management but from aiding the public sector in every country to do its job.

The commodification of water is wrong—ethically, environmentally and socially. It ensures that decisions regarding the allocation of water would center on commercial, not environmental or social justice considerations. Privatization means that the management of water resources is based on principles of scarcity and profit maximization rather than long-term sustainability. Corporations are dependent on increased consumption to generate profits and are much more likely to invest in the use of chemical technology, desalination, marketing and water trading than in conservation.

Depending on desalination technology is a Faustian bargain. It is prohibitively expensive, highly energy intensive—using the very fossil fuels that are contributing to global warming—and produces a lethal byproduct of saline brine that is a major cause of marine pollution when dumped back into the oceans at high temperatures.

A New Water Ethic

The antidote to water commodification is its decommodification. Water must be declared and understood for all time to be the common property of all. In a world where everything is being privatized, citizens must establish clear perimeters around those areas that are sacred to life and necessary for the survival of the planet. Simply, governments must declare that water belongs to the earth and all species and is a fundamental human right. No one has the right to appropriate it for profit. Water must be declared a public trust, and all governments must enact legislation to protect the freshwater resources in their territory. An international legal framework is also desperately needed.

It is strikingly clear that neither governments nor their official global institutions are going to rise to this challenge. This is where civil society comes in. There is no more vital area of concern for our international movement than the world's freshwater crisis. Our entry, point is the political question of the ownership of water; we must come together to form a clear and present opposition to the commodification and cartelization of the world's freshwater resources. . . .

Steps needed for a water-secure future include the adoption of a Treaty Initiative to Share and Protect the Global Water Commons: a guaranteed "water lifeline"—free clean water every day for every person as an inalienable political and social right; national water protection acts to reclaim and preserve freshwater systems; exemptions for water from international trade and investment regimes; an end to World Bank- and IMF-enforced water privatizations; and a Global Water Convention that would create an international body of law to protect the world's water heritage based on the twin cornerstones of conservation and equity. A tough challenge indeed. But given the stakes involved, we had better be up to it.

Periodical Bibliography

The following articles have been selected to supplement the diverse views presented in this chapter.

Arun Agrawal and Maria Carmen Lemos	"A Greener Revolution in the Making?: Environmental Governance in the 21st Century," *Environment*, June 2007.
Linda Baker	"Great Big Green Monster Mansions," *Salon.com*, July 7, 2004.
Lester R. Brown	"Picking Up the Tab," *USA Today Magazine*, May 2007.
Dave Brian Butvill	"Make Saving Nature Profitable," *Sierra*, July/August 2004.
Rodger Doyle	"The Lion's Share," *Scientific American*, April 2005.
Economist	"Clean Water Is a Right," November 9, 2006.
Pete Engardio with Kerry Capell and John Carey	"Beyond the Green Corporation," *Business Week*, January 29, 2007.
John Gray	"Geopolitics and the Limits of Growth," *Globalist*, March 17, 2004.
Marc Gunther	"Is Water a Human Right?" *Huffington Post*, June 11, 2007.
Robert F. Kennedy Jr.	"What Must Be Done," *Rolling Stone*, June 28, 2007.
Richard Lacayo	"A New Plan for the Planet," *Time*, March 26, 2007.
Jessica Vascellaro	"Green Groups See Potent Tool in Economics," *Wall Street Journal*, August 23, 2005.
Adam Wiskind	"Cuba: Sustainability Pioneer?" *World Watch*, July/August 2007.

For Further Discussion

Chapter 1

1. Since the gasoline crisis of the 1970s, many energy analysts have warned that the world's oil supply cannot keep pace with the growing demand. According to these observers, most oil wells are at peak capacity and will soon exhaust the major oil deposits on which the world depends. Jad Mouawad, however, offers a more hopeful vision of future oil supplies. He states that industry technology will help locate untapped reserves and that more efficient oil extraction will keep supplies in pace with demand for a long time. Do you think Mouawad's assessment is too optimistic? If so, explain why you think his views are inaccurate. If you think his opinion is viable, what evidence can you find to support this view?

2. Lester Brown argues that food production in the world is falling because of changes to climate and the depletion of water tables. Roger Thurow and Jay Solomon, on the other hand, state that food production is high but the world lacks the means and commitment to distribute it to the impoverished millions who need it most. After reading both viewpoints, which do you think is the greater threat to future generations—food shortages or food distribution? Using ideas and opinions from both articles, explain your answer.

3. After reading the viewpoints by Steve Lonergan and Asit K. Biswas, explain what opinions about current and future water supplies they have in common. Then detail the ways in which their views about a potential water crisis differ.

Do you strongly agree with either analyst's opinion, or does your own view about the topic of water scarcity lie somewhere in between? Explain.

Chapter 2

1. Andre Leu suggests that organic farming can meet the world's food demands, while Ronald Bailey doubts this claim. After reading both viewpoints, decide which opinion you favor and detail the most compelling evidence that convinced you to take your stand and explain why the opposing claims seem less believable.

2. Jeffrey Smith argues that the benefits of genetically modified (GM) foods may not outweigh their potential risks. He asserts that because they have only been around for a relatively short time, no one can be sure of the possible long-term dangers associated with eating GM foods. Taking Smith's view, several African countries have refused shipments of genetically modified foods from the United States because they fear that their nations are being used as testing laboratories and dumping grounds for "Frankenfoods" not wanted by the developed world. The African American Environmentalist Association (AAEA), however, maintains that GM foods should be welcomed in Africa where millions starve due to famine and poor nutrition. After doing some research on the reasons African nations have given for refusing GM food aid, decide whether you think these nations made the right choice. Explain how you reached your conclusion.

3. Emma Duncan charges the world's aquaculture industry with depleting wild feeder fish stocks for use as food for captive fish, leading to potentially irreversible damage. The UN Food and Agriculture Organization states that aquaculture can be made less environmentally destructive if stronger regulations were in place to preserve sustainability and limit the damage to local habitats. Duncan

agrees that stronger regulations are needed but fears the damage has already been done to many wild stocks of fish. Using the information in these viewpoints (and from other sources you can locate), explain whether you think regulation will help the problem of overexploitation.

Chapter 3

1. Currently, most nations experimenting with wind power receive less than 10 percent of their energy needs from this source. Joseph Florence predicts that in some areas this percentage will double in coming decades. After reading the viewpoints by both Florence and Eric Rosenbloom, decide if you think Florence's prediction will come to pass. Citing evidence from the viewpoints, explain why you think wind power is a viable energy alternative for the United States in particular and the world in general.

2. Read the pro-ethanol viewpoint by Vinod Khosla and the opposing view by James Jordan and James Powell. List the pros and cons of embracing ethanol as an alternative energy source as the authors explain them. Then, clarify whether you believe ethanol could become a useful—even dominant—energy source to replace gasoline.

Chapter 4

1. Morgan J. Poliquin argues that "sustainable development" is a term that implies powerful nations and capitalist interests imposing their will upon private businesses and individuals and telling these entities how to use (or not use) the resources they own. While Poliquin is specifically discussing state regulations, he does say that these are coming into use worldwide. In looking at sustainable development as an international practice, James D. Wolfensohn states that regulations and incentives are being used on a global scale to preserve ecosystems and reduce pollution.

Explain how Poliquin would view the methods advocated by the World Bank. Then, decide if you think sustainable development is a worthwhile goal for the international community or whether it is a practice that could do more harm than good. Explain your answer.

2. After reading all the viewpoints in this chapter, formulate a possible course that the world could take to preserve and distribute resources (such as food, water, and oil). In framing your answer, address the concerns of Deborah James, Maude Barlow, and Tony Clarke that multinational corporations are currently dictating how resources are used. Do you see a way to overcome their concerns, or is the current practice of globalization an equitable way to distribute resources? Perhaps, like Rajesh Makwana, you believe that the sum of the world's resources should be equitably shared. How could this be accomplished? Whatever plan you put forth for preserving and distributing global resources, explain its operation and advantages thoroughly.

Organizations to Contact

The editors have compiled the following list of organizations concerned with the issues debated in this book. The descriptions are derived from materials provided by the organizations. All have publications or information available for interested readers. The list was compiled on the date of publication of the present volume; the information provided here may change. Be aware that many organizations may take several weeks or longer to respond to inquiries, so allow as much time as possible.

Center for Global Food Issues
P.O. Box 202, Churchville, VA   24421-0202
(540) 337-6354 • fax: (540) 337-8593
e-mail: cgfi@rica.net
Web site: wwwcgfi.org

The Center for Global Food Issues (CGFI) employs a global perspective in researching and analyzing the agricultural and environmental issues associated with farming. The center promotes free trade and innovative farming technologies in addition to raising awareness about the effect of different farming methods on the environment. CGFI works to ensure sustainability of the global agriculture industry while keeping environmental conservation a central focus. Back issues of the center's publication, *Global Food Quarterly*, are available on its Web site, as are current reports on topics such as organic farming.

Competitive Enterprise Institute
1001 Connecticut Ave. NW, Suite 1250
Washington, DC   20036
(202) 331-1010 • fax: (202) 331-0640
e-mail: info@cei.org
Web site: www.cei.org

The Competitive Enterprise Institute (CEI) is a public policy institute that advocates for the use of free market principles and limited government involvement in addressing national regulatory issues such as environmental policy. The institute promotes the idea that the private sector can provide appropriate and applicable policies to protect the environment. Subscriptions to e-newsletters such as the weekly *EnviroWire* and the *Monthly Planet* are available on CEI's Web site. Past articles, op-eds, and other reports can be found there as well.

Environmental Defense

257 Park Ave. South, New York, NY   10010
(212) 505-2100 • fax: (212) 505-2375
Web site: www.environmentaldefense.org

Founded in 1967, Environmental Defense is a nonpartisan, nonprofit organization that works in cooperation with major corporations to provide solutions to environmental problems. Environmental Defense's campaigns include efforts to fight global warming, protect the oceans, and ensure that U.S. farm policy is beneficial to farmers, consumers, and the environment in the United States and worldwide. Publications such as the *2006 Annual Report* and fact sheets on topics such as farming projects and global warming are available on the Web site.

Greenpeace USA

702 H Street, NW, Washington, DC   20001
(202) 462-1177
e-mail: info@wdc.greenpeace.org
Web site: www.greenpeace.org

Greenpeace is a global organization that employs controversial techniques to raise awareness about environmental issues such as the destruction of ancient forests and the devastation of the world's oceans. Greenpeace opposes the use of nuclear power and the genetic engineering of food crops. Press releases and reports organized by campaign can be found on the organization's Web site.

Hudson Institute
1015 15th St. NW, 6th Floor, Washington, DC   20005
(202) 974-2400 • fax: (202) 974-2410
e-mail: info@hundson.org
Web site: www.hudson.org

The Hudson Institute is a research organization focusing on issues relating to global security, prosperity, and freedom. The institute works to influence and aid global policy makers and business leaders in areas such as human rights and agricultural and biotechnology policy. Publications of the Hudson Institute include the book *Saving the Planet with Pesticides and Plastic* as well as numerous articles, reports, and white papers available on the organization's Web site.

International Food Policy Research Institute
2033 K St. NW, Washington, DC   20006-1002
(202) 862-5600 • fax: (202) 467-4439
e-mail: ifpri@cgiar.org
Web site: www.ifpri.org

The International Food Policy Research Institute (IFPRI) works in cooperation with fifteen organizations worldwide, all supported by the Consultative Group on International Agricultural Research, to research and establish policies that ensure a sustainable food supply and alleviate hunger for the global population. The institute supports the use of genetically modified crops to alleviate hunger and malnutrition, but also supports risk-assessment programs and regulations that ensure the crops are safe for people and the environment. IFPRI publishes books, newsletters, and reports assessing current policies and technologies relating to food availability worldwide.

National Center for Appropriate Technology
3040 Continental Dr., Butte, MT   59701
(406) 494-4572 • fax: (406) 494-2905
e-mail: information@ncat.org
Web site: www.ncat.org

Founded in 1976, the National Center for Appropriate Technology (NCAT) addresses the needs of the poor by providing affordable, innovative technologies to create sustainable agriculture, communities, and energy in the United States. NCAT uses outreach and educational publications to help the public become more aware of possible solutions to today's energy problems. *ACTION* is the quarterly newsletter of NCAT, and the Center manages the National Sustainable Agriculture Information Service, which provides information about water and pest management as well as organic farming.

National Resource Defense Council
40 West 20th St., New York, NY   10011
(212) 727-2700 • fax: (212) 727-1773
e-mail: nrdcinfo@nrdc.org
Web site: www.nrdc.org

The National Resource Defense Council (NRDC) is an environmental action organization dedicated to preserving the environment and its resources for the current generation and those to come. NRDC campaigns include promotion of alternatives to oil such as sustainable biofuels, slowing the effects of global warming, and aiding China in reducing its output of pollutants. Reports, papers, fact sheets, and current legislation concerning these issues and others are available on the organization's Web site.

Organic Farming Research Foundation
PO Box 440, Santa Cruz, CA   95061
(831) 426-6606 • fax: (831) 426-6670
e-mail: info@ofrf.org
Web site: www.ofrf.org

The Organic Farming Research Foundation (OFRF) has been working since 1992 to promote the use of organic farming practices nationwide. By awarding grants for research to improve organic farming and providing accessible research results to the public and policy makers, OFRF has increased awareness of the benefits of these farming methods. Surveys conducted by the foundation, such as the *National Organic Farmers' Surveys* and reports such as *State of the States: Organic Farming Systems Research at Land Grant Institutions 2001–2003*, provide new information about organic farming. In addition, the OFRF newsletter, *Information Bulletin*, offers information about current projects.

Organization of Petroleum Exporting Countries
Obere Donaustrasse 93, Vienna   A-1020
   Austria
Web site: www.opec.org

Headquartered in Austria, the Organization of the Petroleum Exporting Countries (OPEC) is a membership organization representing twelve of the top oil producing countries in the world. Its mission is that of stabilizing prices of oil for producers and ensuring that consumer countries are guaranteed a stable supply of petroleum. Publications containing current information about the state of the oil industry can be found on OPEC's Web site, including the *Monthly Oil Market Report*, the *World Oil Outlook*, and the *OPEC Bulletin*.

People for the Ethical Treatment of Animals
501 Front St., Norfolk, VA   23510
(757) 662-PETA (7382) • fax: (757) 662-0457
Web site: www.peta.org

People for the Ethical Treatment of Animals (PETA), the largest animal rights organization in the world, works to ensure that the rights of animals are observed worldwide. The organization addresses the rights of all animals, and has addressed numerous issues associated with fish farming, including the environmental impact as well as the associated health issues. Details and reports regarding fish farming can be found at the PETA sponsored Web site www.fishinghurts.com/FishFarms.asp.

Political Economy Research Center
2048 Analysis Dr., Suite A, Bozeman, MT   59718

(406) 587-9591
e-mail: perc@perc.org
Web site: www.perc.org

The Political Economy Research Center (PERC) pioneered the principles of free market environmentalism and continues to advocate for this approach to conservation today. Through research, outreach, and education initiatives, PERC promotes the ideas that, with the use of market incentives and accountability regulations, the private sector will serve as a more successful protector of the environment than the government. *PERC Reports* is the organization's quarterly publication. Articles from this journal and other guides, op-eds, and educational materials are on PERC's Web site.

Reason Foundation

3415 S. Sepulveda Blvd., Suite 400, Los Angeles, CA   90034
(310) 391-2245 • fax: (310) 391-4395
Web site: www.reason.org

The Reason Foundation, a libertarian organization, advocates the use of principles such as individual liberty, free markets, and the rule of law in addressing matters of U.S. and global policy. Reason encourages limited government regulation on issues such as air quality, environmental protection, and energy production. The organization instead favors the will of private corporations to solve the environmental, resource related problems facing the world today. The foundation publishes the monthly magazine *Reason* and has many newsletters and commentaries available on its Web site.

Stockholm Environment Institute

11 Curtis Ave., Somerville, MA   02144
(617) 627-3786 • fax: (617) 449-9603
Web site: www.sei.se

The Stockholm Environment Institute (SEI) is an international research institute dedicated to developing and promoting sustainable development strategies worldwide. Established by the Swedish government, the organization has offices worldwide to address issues specific to certain countries and to propose innovative solutions for the rest of the globe. Programs of the institute include focuses on climate and energy, future sustainability, and water resources and sanitation. SEI publishes books such as *Environmental Policy Integration in Practice* and reports such as *Biomass, Livelihoods and International Trade*. Links to specific information about water resource and energy planning projects are on the institute's Web site.

Sustainable Energy Coalition
6930 Carroll Ave., Suite 340, Takoma Park, MD   20912
Web site: www.sustainableenergycoalition.org

The Sustainable Energy Coalition (SEC) was founded in 1992 to provide a central advocacy network for individuals and organizations concerned about the use of unsafe energy resources that pollute the environment. SEC has since worked to promote the use of energy-efficient, renewable energy sources, and advocates for policies that support electric utility restructuring, pollution prevention, and control of climate change. "Factoids" detailing studies on renewable energy sources, such as biomass and wind power, are available on SEC's Web site.

World Bank
1818 H St. NW, Washington, DC   20433
(202) 473-1000 • fax: (202) 477-6391
e-mail: pic@worldbank.org
Web site: www.worldbank.org

The World Bank is comprised of two institutions, the International Bank for Reconstruction and Development (IBRD) and the International Development Association (IDA). The IBRD provides financial assistance to middle-income countries or poor countries who qualify for credit, while the IDA works with the countries suffering the greatest amount of poverty. Using these two institutions, the World Bank strives to reduce poverty and improve living standards worldwide. Research on how to achieve these goals focuses on topics such as sustainable rural and urban development, and reports such as *Toxic Agriculture Pollution: An Emerging Story* highlight the importance of resource availability in driving development. The World Bank Web site makes this and other reports available online.

Worldwatch Institute
1776 Massachusetts Ave. NW, Washington, DC   20036-1904
(202) 452-1999 • fax: (202) 296-7365
e-mail: worldwatch@worldwatch.org
Web site: www.worldwatch.org

The Worldwatch Institute is a research organization dedicated to providing accessible information on environmental, social, and economic issues to the public. With publications such as the annual *State of the World* and *Vital Signs*, the bi-monthly magazine *Worm Watch*, and other print resources, the organization funds one-third of its initiatives and educates individuals worldwide. The main goal of the institute is to achieve "an environmentally stable and socially just society."

Bibliography of Books

Terry L. Anderson and Donald R. Leal — *Free Market Environmentalism.* New York: Palgrave, 2001.

Wilfred Beckerman — *A Poverty of Reason: Sustainable Development and Economic Growth.* Oakland, CA: Independent Institute, 2003.

Godfrey Boyle, ed. — *Renewable Energy.* New York: Oxford University Press, 2004.

Travis Bradford — *Solar Revolution: The Economic Transformation of the Global Energy Industry.* Cambridge, MA: MIT Press, 2006.

Lester R. Brown — *Outgrowing the Earth: The Food Security Challenge in the Age of Falling Water Tables and Rising Temperatures.* New York: W. W. Norton & Co., 2005.

Gordon Conway — *The Doubly Green Revolution: Food for All in the Twenty-first Century.* Ithaca, NY: Cornell University Press, 1999.

Kenneth S. Deffeyes — *Beyond Oil: The View from Hubbert's Peak.* New York: Hill and Wang, 2005.

Paul Driessen — *Eco-Imperialism: Green Power, Black Death.* Bellevue, WA: Free Enterprise Press, 2003.

Leslie A. Duram   *Good Growing: Why Organic Farming Works.* Lincoln: University of Nebraska Press, 2005.

Howard Geller   *Energy Revolution: Policies for a Sustainable Future.* Washington, DC: Island Press, 2003.

Peter Huber   *Hard Green: Saving the Environment from the Environmentalists: A Conservative Manifesto.* New York: Basic Books, 1999.

Peter W. Huber and Mark P. Mills   *The Bottomless Well: The Twilight of Fuel, the Virtue of Waste, and Why We Will Never Run Out of Energy.* New York: Basic Books, 2005.

Michael T. Klare   *Resource Wars: The New Landscape of Global Conflict.* New York: Metropolitan Books, 2001.

Paul Kristiansen, Acram Taji, and John Reganold, eds.   *Organic Agriculture: A Global Perspective.* Ithaca, NY: Comstock, 2006.

Paul Kruger   *Alternative Energy Resources: The Quest for Sustainable Energy.* Hoboken, NJ: Wiley, 2006.

Bill Lambrecht   *Dinner at the New Gene Café: How Genetic Engineering Is Changing What We Eat, How We Live, and the Global Politics of Food.* New York: St. Martin's Press, 2002.

Richard Manning — *Against the Grain: How Agriculture Has Hijacked Civilization*. New York: North Point, 2004.

Richard Manning — *Food's Frontier: The Next Green Revolution*. New York: North Point, 2000.

Adrian Myers — *Organic Futures: A Case for Organic Farming*. White River Junction, VT: Chelsea Green, 2006.

Fred Pearce — *When the Rivers Run Dry: Water, the Defining Crisis of the Twenty-first Century*. Boston: Beacon, 2006.

Peter Pringle — *Food, Inc.: Mendel to Monsanto—The Promises and Perils of the Biotech Harvest*. New York: Simon & Schuster, 2005.

Paul Roberts — *The End of Oil: On the Edge of a Perilous New World*. Boston: Houghton Mifflin, 2005.

Anita Roddick with Brooke Shelby Biggs, eds. — *Troubled Water: Saints, Sinners, Truth and Lies About the Global Water Crisis*. White River Junction, VT: Chelsea Green, 2004.

Vandana Shiva — *Earth Democracy: Justice, Sustainability, and Peace*. Cambridge, MA: South End Press, 2005.

Matthew R. Simmons — *Twilight in the Desert: The Coming Saudi Oil Shock and the World Economy*. Hoboken, NJ: Wiley, 2005.

R. David Simpson, Michael A. Toman, & Robert U. Ayres, eds.	*Scarcity and Growth Revisited: Natural Resources and the Environment in the New Millennium.* Washington, DC: Resources for the Future, 2005.
Vaclav Smil	*Energy at the Crossroads: Global Perspectives and Uncertainties.* Cambridge, MA: MIT Press, 2005.
William Sweet	*Kicking the Carbon Habit: Global Warming and the Case for Renewable and Nuclear Energy.* New York: Columbia University Press, 2006.
Peter Tertzakian	*A Thousand Barrels a Second: The Coming Oil Break Point and the Challenges Facing an Energy Dependent World.* New York: McGraw-Hill, 2006.
Colin Tudge	*Feeding People Is Easy.* Grosseto, Italy: Pari, 2007.
Felicia Wu and William Butz	*The Future of Genetically Modified Crops: Lessons from the Green Revolution.* Santa Monica, CA: RAND, 2004.

Index